Surrender It, Sis!

It's Time For Your Next Chapter.

Curated By

Apostle
Vicki Gregory-Johnson

SURRENDER IT, SIS!
It's time for your Next Chapter.

Copyright © 2025 Healing Press Publications LLC.

Booking | Speaking | Podcast Engagements
Contact us at: healingpresspublications@gmail.com

ISBN: 979-8-9900123-2-5

All rights reserved. No part of this publication may be reproduced, distributed, or transmitted in any form, such as photocopying, recording, or any other methods, without prior written permission from the publisher.

Publishing Contact Info:
healingpresspublications@gmail.com

Six Ladies With A Message of Hope, Healing And Victory!

Life can be a "pill". In today's world, what's NOT pulling on you? A few of us have discovered that surrounding ourselves with healthy people can make a huge difference. Surrender It, Sis! was written by **six down-to-earth ladies** who have all overcome in some way. We have now combined our life-giving words to push you up and into your due season of victory!

Every lady, every voice, and every word will teach you to release the feminine champion that God has placed inside of you. Society teaches that greatness is about what or who you control. Christ teaches us that greatness comes through surrender. What you hold on to, will eventually hold on to you!

It's your turn.

Surrender It, Sis!
"It's time for your Next Chapter.

Table of Contents

(Six Powerful Voices)

Co-Author
Rev. Beverly L. Smith, MMin. — 9

Co-Author
Apostle, Vicki Gregory-Johnson, DMin. — 25

Co-Author
Lady Shenise L. Smith — 49

Co-Author
Sis. Tisha M. Clay, M.S., Ed/M.A. Ed. — 77

Co-Author
Prophetess Lenette Davidson, MMin. — 105

Co-Author
Sis. Hil Avery — 125

It's time for your Next Chapter.

Surrender It, Sis!

Co-Author
Rev. Beverly L. Smith, MMin.

    Come on in the room, Sis, have a seat, and take a load off; so, we can talk about this thing called "ISSUES" of life. Proverbs 4:23 NKJV Keep your heart with all diligence, for out of it spring the issues of life. I love how it's also written in the Message Bible; Keep vigilant watch over your heart; that's where life starts. What is it that has you bound, feeling defeated, and has kept you from reaching your divine destiny and purpose in life? What are the issues of your heart that are flowing and keeping you awake at night with anxiety?

    The issues that keep you spinning the block day in and day out, back and forth into a vicious cycle of emptiness, loneliness, toxic relationships, infidelity, unresolved childhood traumas-sexual abuse, domestic violence, psychological and mental abuse, abandonment issues.

    Which one of these issues is weighing you down and

has you in a state of stagnation in life? What rottenness is eroding you underneath this exterior? What is the root cause of all this suppressed pain? Have you ever met someone who appears to be stand-offish and so guarded that they are reluctant to speak even when they are spoken to, that is, until you really get to know them deep inside? This is the case for many women who are guarded and have trust issues due to these types of heart-related issues and trauma bonds.

    Always guarded and on the defense like a lioness in stealth position, ready to strike at any moment to defend her territory in order to keep everyone out. It's this silo or wall of protection and defense mechanism that she has built up for herself. How many of us, if we're completely honest with ourselves, can testify to being one of these women? I know I most certainly can. I, too, am one of these women who was broken, bruised, and forsaken. Yet even in the midst of brokenness, guilt, and shame, our Lord in the Power of his Sovereignty will always prevail and get the Glory.

    I know some of you are wondering, while in the valley of deep, traumatizing hurt, where is God, and how can he get the Glory when I'm the one in this agonizing and excruciating heart pain. Let me encourage you by sharing, he's RIGHT THERE! I recall having a conversation with God and asking him why he allowed me to go through what I experienced as a child, and his answer to me was, It wasn't for you, it was for my Glory and my Benefit. I said, Lord, how can I, who was resented as a child simply for being born versus being revered, when I was supposed to be a blessing and not a burden. Conceived in sin, never told who my father was, although I've since learned of him through Ancestry; none of this was of my choosing. Where is the Glory in that?

He then reminded me, according to his word in Jeremiah 1:5 AMP, "Before I formed you in the womb, I knew you [and approved of you as My chosen instrument], And before you were born, I consecrated you [to Myself as My own]. Unlike Moses, God didn't stutter; he was very concise and very intentional when he created, formed, and shaped me for himself.

Notice in the text he said I referring to Himself three times and My twice. Psalm 27:10 When my father and my mother forsake me, then the LORD will take care of me. Psalm 139:14 Fearfully and Wonderfully made. It was at this moment that I became enlightened and completely understood why God had chosen me for HIS Glory. "I Surrendered It." I had my power back. The truth of the matter is, we are all chosen by God and for His glory. He has a plan for each and every one of us, regardless of the heartaches and pain that life brings, and suffering for his sake is part of it. 1Peter 5:10 ESV And after you have suffered a little while, the God of all grace, who has called you to his eternal glory in Christ, will himself restore, confirm, strengthen, and establish you.

It's all part of his plan, Jeremiah 29:11 For I know the plans and thoughts that I have for you says the Lord, plans for peace and well-being and not for disaster, to give you a future and a hope. As much as you'd like to think that you're the only one going through the issues that are flowing from

Surrender It, Sis!

your heart, I can assure and attest that you're not the only one. I know all too well that it's a debilitating and isolated feeling, as though you are walking in this thing all alone. I recall several years ago, I went to a women's conference by myself. I found this conference listed on Eventbrite. I didn't tell a soul I was going; I didn't invite or ask anyone to go with me, I wanted to go alone and spend the afternoon with the Lord, just doing me; to hear some uplifting, empowering words and motivation from some like-minded sisters in Christ. That's it, that's all, nothing else.

When I arrived, it was a small, intimate church with a nice turnout of women seeking the same thing; however, I didn't know a soul there. I did recognize one older lady from my current church who also attended; we at the time didn't know each other, although we did recognize one another. The host for the conference had this elaborate agenda all planned out, typed up, and ready to go, that is, until her printer died the night before. Therefore, she wasn't able to print off the programs for the event because God had greater plans. She said I became so frustrated. Then she said the Lord spoke to her and said, "You will not need that agenda." He told her to talk, fellowship with the ladies, and have service, and that's exactly what she did. When I tell you the power of the Holy Ghost came through like a mighty wind, so many women who had been held captive for years were set free that day.

Some shared their testimony of how they overcame drug and alcohol abuse, prostitution, rape, and molestation. One lady had served time in prison for murdering her abuser, and not one person in her church knew. These weren't just your everyday run-of-the-mill women; these were saved, delivered, and born again, baptized believers who were mothers, grandmothers, widows, daughters, sisters, aunts, nieces, and cousins, all singing in the choir or serving on the usher board, deaconesses, Women Preachers, and Pastor wives.

Some of these women were college-educated women who held leadership positions in various congregations and corporations. It was the power of these women's testimonies that one woman in her mid-60s was finally set free. John 8:36 So if the Son sets you free, you will be free indeed. For the very first time in her life, with streams of tears rolling down her face, she shared that she was molested by an uncle through marriage to her aunt, starting at the age of four. She was a very smart, inquisitive child who spoke up and told her aunt that he had touched her. The aunt knew, however because this man paid all the bills, provided a roof over their heads and put food on the table; this low life aunt allowed him to have his way with this innocent child by stripping her intentionally of her innocence so that SHE could have a place to live and be financially provided for; no matter the cost or who she had to sacrifice to do it.

She then goes on to tell this little four-year-old girl to keep quiet and never speak of it again. This crushed and broke the very essence of this child spirit; she had to journey through life carrying this heavy-laden burden for over 60 years. Can you imagine the weight she carried knowing that her aunt willingly trafficked her for a meal ticket? To add insult to injury, both the aunt and her rapist husband were still alive and still together on the day of the conference. When the Holy Spirit showed up on that day, this broken and bruised little girl who had been held captive inside this woman for over 60 years was finally set free. "She Surrender It." She had finally taken back and reclaimed her power; the enemy no longer controlled her life, he had been defeated and destroyed. Proverbs 18:10 The name of the Lord is a Strong tower; the righteous run to it and are safe.

She no longer had to worry about her heart condition and how she wanted to avenge and get her life back on track against all those who had fumbled, mishandled, and mistreated the little girl inside her. Jeremiah 17:9 The heart is deceitful above all things and beyond cure. Who can understand it? "I, the LORD, search the heart and examine the mind, to reward each person according to their conduct, according to what their deeds deserve." There are countless women throughout scripture, some named and unnamed, who have experienced and endured these same atrocities and heart issues.

Take Hagar, for instance, in the 16th Chapter of Genesis, vs 1-16, A young slave girl to Sarai, who would later become known as Sarah, the wife of Abraham. Sarai forced this maidservant to sleep with her husband to bare him a son. Once she became pregnant, Sarai despised, rejected, and mistreated her to the point where Hagar ran away into the desert. Sarai resented the fact that Hagar now had first dibs on the birthrights to Abraham's seed. Once in the desert, the Angel of the Lord told Hagar, You must go back to

It's time for your Next Chapter.

your mistress and submit to her.

I couldn't imagine what Hagar must have thought when the Angel initially said GO BACK. Imagine having to go back to a situationship where you are the slave; you obeyed both your mistress and her husband, yet you're the one who gets punished for doing exactly what they asked you to do. That is, until the Angel of the Lord told her, " I will increase your descendants so much that they will be too numerous to count". The Angel also said to her that she would give birth to a son and name him Ishmael, which means God hears. It was at that moment she knew that not only did God hear her but that he sees her. She went on to name God El Roi, the one who sees me. Just like Hagar, no matter your circumstances, El Roi sees you. God is Sovereign; he sees your hurt, pain, anger, resentment, and frustrations; God sees all of you.

Just like with Hagar, even when it hurts or doesn't make any sense, you must trust God's will and plans for your life, no matter how complex or complicated it becomes. Isaiah 46:1-3 But now, thus says the LORD, who created you, O Jacob, And He who formed you, O Israel: "Fear not, for I have redeemed you; I have called you by your name; You are Mine. When you pass through the waters, I will be with you; And through the rivers, they shall not overflow you. When you walk through the fire, you shall not be burned, nor shall the flame scorch you, for I am the LORD your God, The Holy One of Israel, your Savior. There's a song that I love by Elevation Worship called "See A Victory" here is a few versus of the lyrics; The weapon may be formed, but it won't prosper When the darkness falls, it won't prevail Cause the God I serve knows only how to triumph My God will never fail Oh, my God will never fail I'm going to see a victory I'm going to see a victory For the battle belongs to You, Lord I'm going to see a victory I'm going to see a victory For the battle belongs to You, Lord (oh yeah) There's power in the mighty name of Jesus Every war He wages He will win I'm not backing down from any giant Cause I know how this story ends Yes, I know how this story ends.

These lyrics point to that expected end that Jeremiah speaks of. After you have "Surrendered It," we will see and experience the victory. Surrender first by yielding to the Holy Spirit, so that you can become more Christ-like by the renewing of your mind. Romans 12:2 NLT, Don't copy the customs and behaviors of this world, but let God transform you into a new person by changing the way you think. Then you will learn to know God's will for you, which is good and pleasing and perfect. If you're not careful, what didn't break and kill you will now try to control. Do you remember the old commercial from United Negro College Fund (UNCF) that says A Mind Is A Terrible Thing to Waste. It all starts with a mindset change and a willingness to be transformed and renewed. Spend quality and intentional time with the Lord through prayer and the studying of His Word. I can tell you from experience that this could become a journey that you might have to walk alone. What do I mean? I'm glad you asked! When you are being transformed and made anew, everyone cannot go with you. No one can go where the Lord is taking you. You might have to leave some folks or what's familiar and comfortable to you behind. It's part of the pruning and growth process.

You're being elevated to new heights, surroundings, and people. Serving the Lord can sometimes be unorthodox and uncomfortable in his plans for us. The path to your destiny and purpose won't look the same for you as it does for someone else, although the instructions might have some similarities. Surrendering to God is one of the most challenging decisions a believer will ever face. It is the act of placing every aspect of yourself—your thoughts, desires, plans, relationships, future hopes and dreams under God's authority and trusting him completely. This is not passive resignation or giving up on yourself; it is an intentional surrender to align yourself with the will of God, and believing that his plans are perfect even when they differ from what you think they should be. Proverbs 3:5-6 NIV Trust in the LORD with all your heart and lean not on your own understanding; in all your ways submit to him, and he will make your paths straight.

The word "submit" means to give in or yield to God's authority, not out of defeat or weakness, but out of trusting and solely relying on him. Once you submit, that's when you begin to get that calmness and inner peace that surpasses all understanding. Philippians 4:7 ESV And the peace of God, which surpasses all understanding, will guard your hearts and your mind in Christ Jesus. Apart from God, our hearts are restless, but in Him, we find proper rest. Romans 5:1 says, "Therefore, since we have been justified through faith, we have peace with God through our Lord Jesus Christ." This verse tells us that good works do not earn peace with

God but are a gift of grace received through faith in Jesus. We cannot measure true peace; it goes beyond the boundaries of calm. It's that blessed assurance that no matter what life brings, we are safe and secure in our Lord Jesus Christ. Peace comes from knowing that our sins are forgiven, our lives are in His hands. How many of us struggle in finding peace because of guilt, shame, or how we think others perceive us due to our past failures or mistakes, even if it's not our doing? Understanding how peace with God is established and maintained is crucial for living a life of joy and freedom. Peace with God is the state of harmony and reconciliation between humanity and sin.

It means more than just the absence of conflict; it involves trust and a deep relationship with God that must be exercised and carried out daily. Lasting peace with God remains regardless of life's challenges or setbacks; our sins are forgiven; therefore, come what may, we have that blessed assurance in Christ Jesus that through his redemptive blood we have life everlasting. Achieving and maintaining peace with God is important for a fulfilling life. Colossians 1:20 ESV and through him to reconcile to himself all things, whether on earth or in heaven, making peace by the blood of his cross. Peace is rooted in God's character, combining justice, mercy, and faithfulness. Jesus embodies this peace.

While the world often seeks peace through worldly means, God's peace originates from a heart transformed by grace. Trusting in God's promises and submitting to his will sustains you. However, barriers can prevent individuals from experiencing this peace. Unconfessed sin, doubt, pride, and resentment can disrupt our relationship with God. Repentance, faith, and humility help to remove these obstacles. Trusting in God's Word and focusing on positive thoughts, as advised in Philippians 4:8 NLT, and now, dear brothers and sisters, one final thing. Fix your thoughts on what is true, and honorable, and right, and pure, and lovely, and admirable. Think about things that are excellent and worthy of praise. To live in peace with God daily, we must accept Jesus' sacrifice, obey God's commands and follow his instructions, be thankful, practice humility, and pray fervently even when it seems you don't know what to say or ask of him. Isaiah 26:3 reminds us that steadfast trust in God brings perfect peace. Living peacefully with God transforms our lives and relationships, as we are encouraged in Romans 12:18 to promote peace with others.

This peace leads to emotional resilience and the joy of facing adversity more positively. Ultimately, having peace with God ensures our eternal future, allowing us to live fearlessly and be ambassadors of peace to others. Once you have come into his peace by lingering in his presence, that's when you step into the fullness of joy. Psalm 16:11 ESV You make known to me the path of life; in your presence there if fullness of joy; at your right hand and pleasure forevermore. For countless generations, the Psalms have offered peace and strength to those who believe, providing a deep comfort that endures throughout time. Psalm 16, in particular, is rich with love and dedication, resonating strongly with tired travelers seeking rest. Throughout the verses, King David, filled with joy, shows steadfast faith in his Lord as he places his full trust in the God who delivers salvation.

Surrender It, Sis!

The message radiates a comforting assurance, much like a gentle flame that warmly embraces those wandering and longing for peace. The line "in the presence of God there is fullness of joy" shines as a guiding light, providing a sanctuary for weary souls and inviting them to find renewal. This Bible passage highlights David's unwavering trust in God, where he recognizes the Lord as his safe haven and source of joy. Davis was a man who was not perfect by far; he failed God many times, yet he was a man after God's own heart. This particular Psalm of joy shows that genuine happiness arises from being close to God. It cannot be found in material wealth or earthly delights—true joy is rooted in the love and goodness of God. In the English Standard Version of this verse, "eternal pleasures" is interpreted as "pleasures forever." Regardless, joy in God's presence extends beyond our earthly existence. Even when faced with death, God remains faithfully beside us. Though our life's journey may eventually lead us to death, choosing to take joy in God, trusting unwaveringly in Jesus, and fostering the presence of the Holy Spirit within us can lead to boundless joy. This joy transcends our circumstances and infuses every part of who we are, providing a fulfillment and peace that is truly unmatched.

The term "fullness of joy" suggests that being in God's presence offers an extraordinary sense of satisfaction and inner peace that cannot be found elsewhere. It represents a state of complete happiness without any shortage of want or need. Fullness of joy goes beyond mere situations, exceeding temporary feelings or emotions. It fills our entire being, surrounding us with an indescribable sense of pure happiness. However, being close to God does not mean a life free from trials or hardships. Instead, it emphasizes that God's presence provides comfort, strength, and steadfast hope during life's difficulties. This gift from God is not just a momentary pleasure but is everlasting. Unlike life that is fleeting and filled with worldly joys, the fullness of joy found in God's presence is eternal, as it flows from a constant source—God himself.

Our joy and happiness come from the Lord Jesus. We rejoice in the fact that, as Christ's followers, our Savior has freed us from sin and death. Nehemiah 8:10 says that "the joy of the Lord is your strength". As a result, by focusing on Him and His goodness, we may experience great happiness. Through our faith in Jesus Christ, we have been saved from sin and given eternal life. Knowing that we have been brought back to God and have a hope that transcends our earthly existence, this gives us plenty to celebrate. God's Love: As the Bible states, God is love (1 John 4:8). All of God's plans, including the sacrifice of Jesus for us, was love. Understanding God's love for us gives us cause to be happy and joyful, even during difficult circumstances. Being in God's presence gives us a sense of purpose and clear guidance. We may gain clarity and direction by turning to God and discovering pleasure in Him when we are lost or concerned about the future. Consequently, joy in its fullness acts as a guide, directing us toward our true purpose as we define it.

The Bible's timeless message of joy and purpose from

Surrender It, Sis!

God is accessible to all who seek it. By focusing on what actually brings us happiness, we can make the decision to live with intention and purpose. Rather than just going through the motions of everyday life, this entails making decisions that are consistent with our principles and interests. We may embrace God's idea for a meaningful life as we pursue the joy of being in His presence. I love this quote by the late Mother Teresa that says Joy is Prayer; Joy is Strength; Joy is Love; Joy is a net of Love by which you can catch souls. Mother Teresa, a Faithful Servant and Humanitarian, was committed to bringing Joy to those less fortunate, especially widows, orphans, and children. She took great joy and pleasure in doing the Great Commission mandate to bring relief to the suffering, which was her life's work, even when faced with difficulties. People worldwide admired and were inspired by her unwavering devotion and faithfulness. Spending time in prayer and worship helps us connect with the joy that comes from being in God's presence. We are reminded of His kindness and devotion when we concentrate on Him, which fills our hearts with happiness and serenity.

We can express our profound reverence and love for the Almighty by engaging in worship, which is a truly moving experience. We focus all of our attention on the magnificence and splendor of our Creator during these unique times, leaving behind the limitations of our everyday existence. When we wholeheartedly accept the beauty of worship, our spirits are lifted, and we are filled with profound joy, giving us a great sense of tranquility and spiritual contentment.

It's time for your Next Chapter.

Surrender It, Sis!

It's time for your Next Chapter.

Surrender It, Sis!

Co-Author
Apostle, Dr. Vicki Gregory-Johnson

The Eyes of Obedience

Our Life journey will take place with or without approval or permission. Given the array of experiences that will be encountered, it is vital to understand our role and the importance of our participation in this journey. Better days, hmmm, one might ponder. After all I have been through, is it possible to experience God differently? Yes, it is! God is calling you to a place where you can thrive. A place where you actively listen and move, as God says to move. Yes, I hear you saying, "I already do that"! And you are right, but understand, it doesn't stop at one act of obedience, but a lifestyle of obedience. Yes, a new refined place of obedience. Where you truly allow God to be all in all and experience a life of lasting victory.

I'm not saying there won't be mistakes or setbacks, but you will see that they no longer run or ruin your progress. Obeying God refines not only life but also the overall relationship with God. As the building takes place, trusting in God will strengthen you, and your life will begin to produce fruit that will remain—a direction desired and attainable through the power of the Holy Spirit. A call to change the way things are seen. Allowing the eye to be single, focusing on God, refusing all distractions.

This is necessary when you are tired of fleeting victories. You take on the challenge and become willing to take the required risks that may make you look silly to others. Obedience, a desire to please God, will require you to walk away from people, places, and things that connect you to what will not promote progress. What does this kind of obedience look like? It is often wrapped in rejection, misunderstandings, deep-rooted trauma, or even low self-worth. Yes, your victory lies within dysfunction. It will mask itself as a serious problem that is just a symptom. The devil desires that you never discover the root situation, nor understand your role and authority in it. This is where your faith will rise to new heights.

Ultimately, these are the types of things that must be laid aside and surrendered to God. This can often be difficult because what a person is familiar with is commonly sought after. But taking the comfortable route, dwelling where you are familiar, will hold you hostage to what you were given the power to overcome. Taking an active role in obeying God will stretch you beyond life's limitations and uncertainties, causing you to fulfill God's purpose. When you obey God, you say goodbye to familiar things, opening yourself to great possibilities. A journey walked out by faith, that can only be done by trusting in God and obeying him every step of the way. This means that some things will have to change. You must be willing to set and establish guidelines and boundaries. Set parameters in your walk to help develop goals and priorities. This will help build and align oneself with God's will, relying on his divine guidance. Opening up in this area allows the individual's relationship with God to flourish and facilitates the development of strong relationships with others.

Many people refer to this as a tribe. Building on these relationships through the lens of obedience to God creates a dynamic circle. A group of sisters taking the time to surrender what was holding them back, creating a tribe that thrives on pushing other sisters to their potential. You agree to allow the freedom you were given to become contagious, a beautiful winning cycle, where women genuinely help other women. A woman who has taken the time to work on herself and properly heal can benefit others. Isn't this the objective? Heal to help heal.

Firm parameters are nonnegotiable. The Bible instructs us to "guard our hearts with all diligence" (Proverbs 4:23). Ladies, our hearts are the core of who we are, so we must protect them. What you allow in your core is what you become, so be intentional. Monitor your thoughts, where you go, and who you entertain. Take an active role in your progress. This is not a one-time fix, but an ongoing lifestyle of prioritizing God, His ways, and values over convenience and compromise. This will require a firm commitment to your overall development. Pushing you out of your comfort zone and stretching you beyond the unknown.

God's intention for your life is that you win, so take a leap and trust God. Obey him even if it means losing control over what is out of your control. This means surrendering what you thought it should have been. Release yourself from the enemy's plan of constantly looking over your shoulder, looking for something to happen, or wondering why it hasn't happened yet. Instead, rest in Him, knowing that He has everything under control. Watch God move in extraordinary measures on your behalf. You will not regret your yes to God, so don't worry.

Being confident of this very thing, that he which hath begun a good work in you will perform it until the day of Jesus Christ: (Philippians 1:6).

One of the most significant tasks in obeying God is believing Him. Sometimes our obstacles have a louder voice, and navigating through various situations becomes a struggle. It should be simple to obey God, and it is until life's pressures begin to rain on your life. You learn firsthand to trust God and believe Him no matter what comes. Your yes to God becomes a test of your faith and complete loyalty. Don't be afraid, it's time to trust Him, unlike ever before. What are you waiting for? There is greatness on the other side of your obedience.

Wherefore seeing we also are compassed about with so great a cloud of witnesses, let us lay aside every weight, and the sin which doth so easily beset us, and let us run with patience the race that is set before us.. (Hebrews 12:1)

Holiness is the Standard

In today's age, having a standard seems ancient. Everyone seems to do whatever feels good or agrees with the culture. With no fear of God for countless generations, it is challenging to model holiness to those who don't know what that looks like. God's expectation is his holy standard. The goal is to move forward, not allowing the world's inconsistencies to deter you. Although this may sound boring, it is necessary. You must accept God's expectation, surrender, and be set apart, dedicated solely to Him. Challenging right? You must be willing to let go of everything and trust God.

Stop running from your freedom, but rather, embrace what he's secured for you. Don't allow fear to hold you back one more day; the victory is yours.

For God hath not given us the spirit of fear; but of power, and of love, and of a sound mind (2 Timothy 1:7 KJV)

Holiness is essential. This devoted life will serve as an example, reflecting a purity that others will aspire to emulate. As you continue to surrender, God transforms what once hindered you into a platform to reach others. Without pretense, this is a plea to progress toward a life of ongoing surrender to God, giving life to a lasting change in your life and the lives of others. This brings pleasure to God. The more we surrender, the more we mirror God's character.

Furthermore, then we beseech you, brethren, and exhort you by the Lord Jesus, that as ye have received of us how ye ought to walk and to please God, so ye would abound more and more. 1 Thessalonians 4:1 (KJV)

The reality of this brings a profound sense of peace. This is a requirement for believers, reminding us that we are not alone. It is also not a one-time fix for everyone, but a lifestyle pleasing to God and worthy of reward. So, where do we go from here? Where do we start? That is the big question. Surrendering is a fantastic decision, but following through will require consistency, determination, and dedication, leading to holiness. Why is holiness essential? It affects our ability to humble ourselves and recognize our dependence on God. It also affects our capacity to trust and obey God, as well as the overall transformation of the believer. This is why we mustn't treat this subject as regular! It is vital for the life and growth of every believer. It often felt like this only applied to the older saints in the church (an old folks saying, so to speak), but this is not the case.

Follow peace with all men, and holiness, without which no man shall see the Lord: (Hebrews 12:14 KJV)

This will result in a lack of a developed and thriving relationship, which the Father desires. Living a life wholly devoted to God will not only foster a strong relationship with the Father, but it will also reflect the reality of His existence and presence to the world. As we embark on a fantastic future, this is something very important to take seriously and worth striving for! It is a personal, lasting change that provokes change in others. God is Holy; we therefore should be Holy. This standard is attainable and necessary through the working of the power of the Holy Ghost.

Speak unto all the congregation of the children of Israel, and say unto them, Ye shall be holy: for I the LORD your God am holy (Leviticus 19:2 KJV)

Leave it at the Cross

The enemy is notorious for reminding us of our past failures. He reminds us of our unworthiness to experience God's grace, a fight we must engage in daily. Declaring the Word of God over our lives is not merely something to insert into our daily routines; it is a mandate. Embracing the present, detaching from the past, and abandoning all dead things at the cross. This will foster confidence and sustaining strength, which are necessary for an ever-evolving relationship with God.

The power of the cross enables us to experience the freedom to walk through each day in victory. Of course, this is not because we deserve it, but because it was part of Christ's mission and purpose for humanity. Given such an incredible opportunity, it is important not to get sidetracked by the enemy. Staying on course requires an honest self-assessment. Being truthful with oneself is key. This is helpful and will strategically shift your focus away from others' lives, allowing you to focus more attention on your own, and helping you to be exactly where God wants you to be—a place where you can hear clearly with fewer distractions.

The cross is a constant reminder of the Savior and His perfect act of selfless surrender. We can also become Mission-minded, living out our purpose with precision. Knowing that lack and dependency on the approval of man was nailed to the cross along with every other hindrance, for God is our gatekeeper. Although the pressures of life may persist, its power over us shall not prevail.

No weapon that is formed against thee shall prosper; and every tongue that shall rise against thee in judgment thou shalt condemn (Isaiah 54:17 KJV).

Embrace the freedom purchased at the cross. Let us no longer live as slaves to sin. Imagine this: receiving a beautiful gift box but never taking the time to see what's inside. As women, we receive countless gifts throughout our lifetime, so many that it almost becomes common. It can become easy to compare it to others and simply set it aside. Not that you are not appreciative, and you intend to take a more thorough look later, you tell yourself, but you never get to it. With this approach, you will miss out on some amazing things that God had in store. It turns out that it's not just another thoughtful, beautiful gift to add to your collection of thoughtful gifts. You open the box, and you don't find just something, but you find yourself. You continue to

It's time for your Next Chapter.

find a new, refined version of you. The best gift you'll ever receive. Don't mistake this gift for the others; it is precious and continues to give.

Ladies, this is what the cross purchased for us. We can look within ourselves honestly and receive help in our time of need. We discover a place to surrender it all and receive all that He has for us. Comfortable and confident, knowing that He has us safely protected, despite various obstacles or hindrances, we win! No longer walking as victims, but walking in your God-given authority.

This becomes an incredibly miraculous exchange. You can bring all your burdens to the Lord and leave them there, receiving forgiveness and a fresh start. You are no longer hindered by your past or discouraged by the outcome of the future. Instead, have faith in every step you take day by day, trusting God to see you through. You give everything to Him, and He gives you everything you need. It is far more than you can handle, so why wait another day holding on to what you were designed to release? Pressing into what's ahead takes courage, but it is what is required to fulfill God's intended purpose. However, know that you are not alone. The Father promised that He would never leave nor forget you. Clinging to His every word, we carefully move forward, trusting Him to bring forth what we are unable to. With this in mind, this will help us develop and choose our circles wisely. Taking into account what was purchased for us, we begin to move and think differently. Challenged yet confident in yielding a better version of ourselves is not an option, but it is necessary for a healthy, productive life.

Surrender It, Sis!

Unfortunately, not everyone is excited about the changes you are making towards a better you. With this in mind, don't let that stop you. Instead build and protect what you allow around you. Even a computer requires protection from a virus. Even though a person may mean well, if they haven't been healed, their input can be poisonous and can cause a hindrance to your growth. Don't give up on others, love them. But surround yourself with other mission-minded individuals whom you trust to hold you accountable.

This will help you stay focused on the journey ahead and divert your attention away from the obstacles that may arise. Don't be afraid to stretch and grow. But rather, create space for constructive critique as you continue to learn and build on the revised version of yourself. She is ever-evolving, overcoming all odds. This will occur quickly, so be sure to enjoy every moment of this journey, Sis!

True Development

In the busyness of ministry and ever-changing times, it is important to schedule time for yourself. With ongoing concerns and demands that are gladly accepted, they're often put first. However, you must also prioritize making space for yourself. This is not selfish but necessary. You need to take time to be refreshed and enjoy some downtime. In essence, you must surrender even this to God. It is truly a valuable part of positive, active development.

Turn off your phone, ignore any emails, and delay so-

It's time for your Next Chapter.

cial media for now. Use this time to center yourself and resist the urge to respond right away. Respond to your need to reset and feel refreshed. Allow yourself to return to your responsibilities refreshed and with new, clear perspectives. Sis, you do matter, and sometimes you need to be bold enough to remind yourself. You have many wins that you haven't even taken the time to celebrate. Take a moment to step back from your responsibilities, take a deep breath, and take it all in.

Let the Lord carry you into your next season, refreshed and prepared for the tasks ahead. Renewal is essential for growth. This designated time will help expand your capacity and improve your clarity, allowing you to step into new territory with confidence.

Restore unto me the joy of thy salvation, and let a willing spirit sustain me. (Psalm 51:12)

If you are careful, it becomes easier each day to live life as a preview. It looks and feels good, but you can never fully attain it. The enemy can be compelling, to the degree that you believe the delusions he disseminates. The enemy is a liar; "don't believe his lies!" You have the victory, a victory that requires you to submit to and conform to it daily. This walk requires your full-time attention and devotion; the health of your spiritual development depends on it.

Place this at the front of priorities, making each moment count. Victory is guaranteed, but it takes you to seize it. Refuse to live life as a bystander, reviewing what you were meant to live. But, instead, be partakers of the fruit. Surrender does not come naturally; it is a discipline, an act of obedience to God. It is a daily challenge to release one's will and entrust it in God's hands. This level of development will not take place if there is no time spent in the presence of God.

Spending time in prayer will cultivate a close relationship that fosters trust. And the more you trust, the more you will be able to entrust. You will not only learn more about God and His ways, but you will also learn more about your own.

Cast thy burden upon the LORD, and he shall sustain thee: he shall never suffer the righteous to be moved (Psalm 55:22 KJV).

Evaluate your present moment and refuse to return to yesterday's turbulence. You were designed to move "from forward." Just because you moved forward doesn't mean you stop there. Victory defines your lifetime, not just a moment in it. So, looking back or retreating are not options.

Leading doesn't pause to give you a moment to breathe. The gifts and calling of God are a blessing, but the demand is real and requires maturity. As seasoned runners train themselves to breathe effectively during a race, you must do the same. This is a race, and you need to train yourself to live, not just survive.

It can be challenging to focus on what God is saying

or hear Him clearly when balance is missing. But I challenge you to re-establish it right now! Get back on track with what God has placed in your heart. Move now!

Shake the dust off and come out of your comfort zone. Why? Because the time is now! You haven't plateaued, Sis, you've only just begun. You don't have to try to rewrite the story, Sis, but just keep pressing, winning from forward.

But as it is written, Eye hath not seen, nor ear heard, neither have entered into the heart of man, the things which God hath prepared for them that love him.
1 Corinthians 2:9 (KJV)

Surrender and Arise

After many years of facing difficulties and challenges, I gradually realized a deep need for women to be empowered. This empowerment comes through a continuous act of surrender, often in areas women tend to hide or mask. It involves deep-rooted trauma, overlooked until it manifests in her behavior. Her character gradually reveals who she truly is, and her wounds become visible. She not only needs strength but also healing.

Over twenty years as a hairstylist, I heard many stories behind the salon chair—stories of hurt, abuse, struggles, and serious battles that these women were often ashamed to share. As they confidently shared, I listened to each woman who sat in the chair, and the Lord began to show me a need. Adversity was not the end of their story, nor mine. It was more of a wake-up call.

These women endured things they were not comfortable sharing just anywhere. The salon had become a place of healing and release. Ladies would often drive by to pray; it became a place of revival. Some women didn't have a hair appointment, but God met them there. Five years later, my ministry journey began on March 10th, 2005. My relationships with the women continued to grow. We cried, shared, and prayed together. A women's ministry network was developing out of these bonds and ashes.

I retired from the salon many years later, but my desire to reach women in need grew stronger. A few years after that, I shared with my husband the idea of starting a prayer conference call for women. We pondered what to name the women's ministry. We considered several options, and suddenly, "Strengthen My Sister" came to mind.

S.M.S stands for Short Message Service. This was it! In these short, impactful encounters with the women, they received the message that they needed from God. Strengthen My Sister was born under the umbrella of Weapons of Praise TV, an international ministry reaching broken women of all ages worldwide.

The Ministry provides women with a safe space to hear a new message - God's message to them - breaking away from what they are accustomed to hearing. It was okay to have gone through many challenges, but God still had great things in mind for them. A healed version of them was waiting to emerge.

Don't BETRAY her. Don't COMPETE with her. HEAL her! "Because healed women thrive."

Strengthen My Sister held its first women's prayer conference call on September 8th, 2022. Every Thursday evening, the Lord began to use this time to heal and refresh the women who called. In September 2023, Strengthen My Sister had its first in-person women's roundtable gathering. We shed light on some challenges women face with insecurities that cause them to count themselves out.

Jealousy and competition persist among women in the church today, hindering their ability to be healed. God wants us whole. Strengthen My Sister targets these areas, getting to the core of each woman's deficiency. The lack of support and help to emerge from these conditions forces women to cover their wounds and surrender in defeat. The ministry's mission is to redirect women to God's plan and to surrender to it.

"For I know the plans I have for you," says the Lord. "They are plans for good and not for disaster, to give you a future and a hope" (Jeremiah 29:11 NLT)

Refresh and restore women through prayer and the Word of God. Embrace the fact that it is time to get up, arise, come out of hiding, and walk in your God-given purpose. Strengthen My Sister® became an official trademark in March 2025. God continues to groom this community of women. We strengthen and build one another, trusting and believing that all things are possible with God.

With men this is impossible; but with God all things are possible. (Matthew 19:26 KJV)

The time has come to examine the cost of what you expect more closely. There is a high expectation of those you lead. Which is not bad, but are you willing to give what you expect? Before you answer yes, take a moment and ponder that thought for a second. I know you are yet saved, sanctified, filled with the Holy Ghost, and with FIRE. God's leading lady is a faithful, devoted leader of leaders. Hallelujah! But, for a moment, think about this. Do you desire to see more?

More is often desired, but more must be surrendered. I know, most of the answers are yes! I am willing to give. But would you agree it is much easier to say it than to do it? To demonstrate this type of leadership is a challenge that costs more than most are willing to pay.

What does more look like? Embracing more will propel you to Move Outside your Regular Efforts and break fresh ground for the benefit of others. Yes, I know that you have surrendered. You have given much. You seek the Lord earnestly for guidance and direction. But there is more! This journey demands more than regular effort, but the rewards are immeasurable.

It's time for your Next Chapter.

Reach beyond your routine. There is fresh, new ground waiting. When you surrender consistently, you get the same regular results. But when you go to war and push past normal, you open the door to abundance far above all you ask or imagine. Well done, Sis, but it's time to turn the page. It's been a great run, but staying where you are will cost too much. Remember, 'more' is not a destination; it's a journey. And it's a journey worth taking!

Today, let's go beyond our usual routine. Let's surrender more as we guide the next generation into new opportunities. Remember, our actions today shape the future for those who come after us.

Understand, it's not just about you. In today's world, building her can look impossible and overwhelming. "Her": She is your mom, your sister, your daughter, your friend, your neighbor, the woman you have not met yet. A life waiting to be impacted by what God has placed inside you.

Building others has a lot to do with what we say. We know hearing is also very important, but our words can build or tear down.

"Death and Life are in the power of the tongue: and they that love it shall eat the fruit thereof." (Proverbs 18:21 KJV).

As we continue ministering to others, let us use our words carefully; we cannot retract what's been released. Let's be honest! We are talkers, ladies. And truthfully, sometimes we can say too much. So, this is often an area we must watch intentionally for most of us.

Our sisters are hurting, and Her Energy is Relying on you. Your words matter! Take a moment to be concerned and care. Her life today was shaped by words spoken to her yesterday. She is waiting for a word that will attack her insecurities, tear down the walls of limitations, and open new possibilities.

She is waiting for her release date. Could that word, that release date, be coming through you? You can unleash her tomorrow with the very words in your mouth! Build her today! As you're building her, you are also building yourself. Because "Her" is also you.

Speak Life! I encourage you to walk it out, Woman of God. Be strengthened today, for the outcome is far greater than you could imagine. Generations to come are depending on you. Keep speaking into her, building her, and watching God, because His hand is on it.

"I have planted, Apollos watered; but God gave the increase." 1 Corinthians 3:6 KJV.

You will have many encounters and experiences in life that can cause you to lose focus and potentially fall prey to discouragement. However, as time has progressed, you have found that trusting and relying on God has become second nature—the assurance before you causes you to press beyond the pressures of life. There is a reach inside you that keeps pulling, so you welcome the stretch because you know there's more. There is more of you to let go of and more of God to experience.

You've witnessed how life has a way of impinging upon progress. But there's yet a fresh wind, a move of God, a knowing that the ultimate victory is yours no matter how difficult it may seem or become. God has pulled you out of the wreckage and answered a need through you.

Many have been refreshed through your struggles. Somebody came out because you dared to go through. Your journey has not only strengthened your faith but also inspired others to persevere. This alone made the struggles worth it!

Take a moment and rest in this reality. Yes, it could have destroyed you, but God saw something different. You didn't simply stumble into victory; instead, He wrapped you in victory and repelled the announcement of defeat. God set Himself before you and allowed you to plow through each obstacle. He enabled you to come through it and gave you the revelation to move beyond all-natural means.

Surely, you have endured much, and the power that comes from God alone has sustained you. But now, in this season, the enemy's attacks against you have been defeated. The territory that the enemy previously controlled has been reclaimed and surrendered by force.

God has rendered the enemy's position, authority,

and every weapon powerless in your life. This is the power of surrender—a level of obedience where you can actively expect God's presence to be evident in your situation. This will enable you to move forward with confidence.

For God hath not given us the spirit of fear; but of power, and of love, and of a sound mind (2 Timothy 1:7 KJV).

Therefore, there is no need to hold back or fear; every arrow has been shattered, peace is yours, and the victory has already been secured. Be courageous, step into your authority, Sis; trust in God—this territory is yours! You are not just a survivor but a conqueror!

We are troubled on every side, yet not distressed; we are perplexed, but not in despair; Persecuted, but not forsaken; cast down, but not destroyed; Always bearing about in the body the dying of the Lord Jesus, that the life also of Jesus might be made manifest in our body (2 Corinthians 4:8-10 KJV).

Surrender, the Beginning of Order

Ladies, let's face it, when you have been single without clear boundaries, it can be hard to figure out where they fit in your life. As a single person, you might think boundaries aren't necessary. You may have an "I can do whatever I want" and "I don't answer to anybody" attitude. Maybe this would be okay if you were the only one affected by your choices. Not having boundaries can lead to unwanted consequences. This area can be highly challenging. You are single, saved, and waiting on God for your mate, but without order, you set yourself up for unnecessary disorder.

I have set before you life and death, blessings and curses. "Now choose life so that you and your children may live." (Deuteronomy 30:19 NIV).

Healthy boundaries are not meant to control you but to establish protection and limits, protection from outside influences, and limits on the access of others in your life. What others can do and what will not be tolerated. This can become challenging in a relationship, as many feel nothing has to change. You may attempt to bring the old thinking into your relationship, only to reach many areas of confusion and disappointment. You may feel that the problem has nothing to do with you. Certainly, most of us feel that our way of doing things is right.

"Fools think their own way is right, but the wise listen to others." (Proverbs 12:15 NLT).

The lack of proper boundaries leads to poor communication. This breeds speculation in places of insecurity. Many are insecure, but establishing boundaries helps create a secure environment. Yes, boundaries are for Today! Be proactive in your approach to boundaries. Help safeguard your current and future relationships by first detecting and protecting the need. This shows you care and that your relationships matter.

Surrender It, Sis!

"Guard your heart above all else, for it determines the course of your life." (Proverbs 4:23 NLT).

This will help you prioritize others' feelings and not dismiss miscommunication as insecurity or simply something they must deal with. This potentially helps all parties in the relationship heal and grow. A person's approach and response are entirely different when they feel heard. They will open up more because the environment feels safe, making them less susceptible to outside influences or feelings of criticism. Secondly, detach from the old mindset—the assumption that boundaries are not important and certainly not for Today!

"Don't copy the behavior and customs of this world, but let God transform you into a new person by changing the way you think." (Romans 12:2 NLT).

They are for Today and will bring order to other areas of your life. Surrendering everything to God helps establish healthy boundaries. They should be built one decision at a time, choosing what can stay and what must go. Be determined to grow, improve, and mature to better yourself and others. Avoid the temptation to blame others and take responsibility for your actions. Live fully the life God has called you to.

"For we are each responsible for our own conduct." (Galatians 6:5 NLT).

Thirdly, we must develop. Most people desire a big

It's time for your Next Chapter.

win, but many get frustrated while waiting for it. The goal shouldn't be to chase the successive big win, but rather to surrender and make a continuous prayer of "Father, prepare me." In essence, change your mindset, as actual healthy Godlike development takes time. Recognize that every win comes with pressure and responsibilities, and you can learn and grow stronger while you wait.

For all these things do the nations of the world seek after: and your Father knoweth that ye have need of these things. But rather seek ye the kingdom of God; and all these things shall be added unto you (Luke 12:30-31 KJV).

We must stop trying to do things our way. As we grow, there is a constant effort to be heard, seek revenge, and maintain unnecessary control. It's a daily struggle to release these controlling tendencies. The goal is to surrender everything to God each day and let Him take full control of your decisions and life. Trust Him with it all. Yes, I hear you—that's easier said than done. But if you take a moment to consider the overall outcome, surrendering is truly worth it. Since we tend to live in the moment without much thought for the future, God sees our entire life and understands everything we need and provides it. With that knowledge, we can trust Him completely.

I encourage you today not to let waiting cause frustration or doubt, wondering when, Lord. Instead, invite God to shape you during the wait. Immerse yourself in His presence and listen for His guidance. Sis, you don't just want to arrive at this destination, but also to have the wisdom to

Surrender It, Sis!

remain. This is key! It brings glory to God. Surrender it, Sis, and let God grow you.

But as it is written, Eye hath not seen, nor ear heard, neither have entered into the heart of man, the things which God hath prepared for them that love him (1 Corinthians 2:9 KJV).

It's time for your Next Chapter.

Surrender It, Sis!

Co-Author
Lady Shenise L. Smith

Many of us are taught to mask our feelings. We present ourselves as if we are alright, we have it all together. The problem with masking our feelings is that we never deal with them. We cause ourselves to walk through life bound to emotional baggage. This emotional baggage is like spiritual roadblocks keeping us from living life to our full potential. We can go on for years believing that we are healed or we have overcome our past until something happens, and it triggers that thing we tucked away from ourselves. When it is brought to our attention, it is truly a time to surrender it to God so that we can receive our healing and deliverance. Yet many of us are comfortable with our masks and continue on living life bound, never living life full and abundantly.

I know this all too well? I thought that because I raised my children and was able to maintain a nice lifestyle, I had overcome my traumatic childhood. I went to Church, I served, tithed, and felt like I was a good person, but something was lacking. My relationships with people suffered. I convinced myself that it was best to keep my inner circle really small rather than letting people get to know the real me. I often told people I am like a light switch; I can turn you off and block you with the quickness. This thought process was dysfunctional to say the least, and the more I operated in this fashion, the more bridges I burned with people. I justified my actions.

    I truly believed I was doing the right thing by protecting myself. I often ran from situations and any conflict that came my way. You all know the term hurt people hurt people. I had a list of people that I hurt with the lash of my tongue and the immediate dissociation. I turned to drinking as my way to cope with my loneliness. I convinced myself that everyone else was the problem, that I was misunderstood, and that I had to keep my distance. This was surely a tactic of the enemy. He planned to keep me isolated, filled with self-pity, and drinking to cope with the feelings. The more I drank, the further I felt from God's presence. I was a carnal Christian living an unfilled life. This was a cycle in which I wanted to break, but I did not have the courage to face myself, not to mention God. I just did not know where to start. I prayed about it, and one day I received a revelation. In a church sermon, the Pastor said the enemy was after my integrity. I thought about all the times I tried to give a word, and it was not received because I was living a compromised lifestyle. I was able to see that I had a purpose that was not being fulfilled. To truly do God's work, I had to make some changes.

It's time for your Next Chapter.

The enemy was exposed, and now it was time to do something about it. My surrender was more like a process. I gave up what I knew was obvious: I had to stop drinking, but I knew it was much deeper than that. I need to get to the root cause of why I was so unfulfilled. I turned to the word of God, 1 Peter 5:7 Casting all your care upon Him, for he cares for you. I said to myself, God, if you really care for me, help me understand why I am the way that I am. I cannot do this alone, and I need you to show me what to do. My answer did not come right away; it took constant prayer and resisting, but it did come. God revealed to me that I was dealing with the spirits of rejection and abandonment that entered my life as a child when my mother decided to disown me. When I looked back over my life, I could see where this was true. Many of my relationships were sabotaged just to keep from feeling rejected or abandoned. I cried like a baby. I was happy to finally understand what was going on and why I was stuck in such a destructive cycle. Having the knowledge was not enough; it was time to do something about it. I sought out spiritual guidance through my Pastor to talk about what it was like to be rejected and abandoned by my mother. As I talked about my feelings, I recalled how fresh the pain felt; it was like it occurred yesterday. That twelve-year-old showed up to tell her story of how devastating it was to be without the love of her only living parent.

I took my mask off long enough to deal with the pain that I had held onto for most of my life. I surrendered to the pain because I felt I could no longer hold on to it. I can tell you that once you start unraveling the pain, you get the courage to keep going. I began to get curious about what it would feel like to finally let go and be free. Once I released my pain, I asked God to heal my heart. He immediately began to show me how the enemy used this to not only separate me and my mother but to cause unforgiveness to dwell in our hearts. I decided at that moment that the enemy was the culprit, Ephesians 6:12, For we wrestle not against flesh and blood, but against principalities, against powers, against the rulers of the darkness of this world, against spiritual wickedness in high places. I forgave myself, and I forgave my mother. I began to pray for her like never before. If God could reveal to me the tactics of the enemy and heal and deliver me, He could do it for her. Now free from the bondage, I could start again. Never would I suspect that the enemy wanted to destroy the relationships in my life because I had a calling to walk alongside my soon-to-be husband in Ministry.

There was work to be done, and God needed me to agree and walk in alignment so he could use me. When you surrender and let your healing and deliverance come forth, you open up the doors to your blessings. I have built some solid relationships with Sisters and have gone on to join a powerful Sister Strengthening Ministry. I am happily married. None of this would have been possible if I had continued down the path I was walking. As disciples of Christ, our goal is to surrender our lives to God and allow the Holy Spirit to guide us in being an example of Christ. Our light is supposed to shine in the midst of darkness, providing hope to a lost world. Matthew 5 14-16. Child of God, you are remarkable, and how you process things that happened to you should be different from those who do not know Jesus. Surrendering is a moment-by-moment reality to any believer who is striving to walk in alignment with the will of God. There is a constant self-evaluation that takes place in our hearts. There is a continuous repentance that occurs, and the outcome should be a constant shift in the right direction. What makes this journey of surrendering beautiful is that you do not look like what you have gone through once you are on the other side of it. I encourage you today to let go of it, Sis. The act of letting go is something we all must do to mature in Christ. The Bible tells us in 2 Corinthians 5:17 Therefore, if any man be in Christ, he is a new creature: old things have passed away; behold, all things have become new.

Because of the blood shed for our sins, once we come to accept Christ, a conversion takes place, and our viewpoints change. As our viewpoints change, we begin to let go of things that do not serve this new life we are living. The Holy Spirit, who is now present within us, convicts us and helps us see what sinful nature we are still holding onto. He is our help in surrendering what needs to die off for us to grow in Christ. These things can be relationships, addictions, these things can also be old ways of thinking, harboring unforgiveness, and selfishness. The point is to be reminded that we are new creatures; the old must pass away. God has his way of cutting things off until we let go. I remember the constant feeling of being unfulfilled and stuck. This feeling lasted for years because I chose to ignore the Holy Spirit's tug at my heart to make a change. I kept looking at the people in my life and blaming them for my actions. I labeled myself misunderstood just to keep holding onto the belief that nothing was wrong with me; it was everybody else. The enemy is cunning; he will trick you into believing a lie just to keep you bound. I know God allowed it so that I would come to the point where I could not take it any longer.

Surrendering is coming to the point where you see that your way of dealing with the matter is not effective. You let go and give it to God for him to restore you. Sometimes the act of letting go involves some additional work. My Husband and I counsel married couples. On many occasions, couples come to us at a point where their marriage is failing and they are considering divorce. What we find is that there has been so much that has happened that resentment has set in and driven a wedge between them. The hardest part of getting them to a place of reconciliation is getting them to surrender their feeling of unforgiveness. Unforgiveness is the leading tactic of the enemy to hold people in bondage.

Many people can go their entire lives holding onto Grudges. The Bible tells us in Ephesians 4:32 Be kind and compassionate to one another, forgiving one another, just as Christ forgave you. As disciples of Christ, we are to forgive not when it is easy but in all circumstances. Jesus told Peter in Matthew 18: 21-22 Then came Peter to him, and said, Lord, how oft shall my brother sin against me, and I forgive him? till seven times? Jesus saith unto him, I say not unto thee, Until seven times: but, until seventy times seven. I have to believe that God knew if we did not forgive, our hearts would become so hardened that we would not be able to hear from the Holy Spirit. Our hearts need to be pliable to surrender. The more people focus on the offense and the feelings associated with it, the harder it is to let go and forgive. Once you allow yourself to forgive the offense, you can surrender the pain associated with it and receive your healing.

The act of letting go takes effort, but healing, deliverance, and restoration are in store for those who are willing to do the work. How sweet it is to defeat the enemy and to be able to take a break in your life. The more you let go, the more ground you gain. Our goal as believers is to be the example of Christ, and our fruits bear witness. Mathew 5:17 Even so, every good tree bears good fruit, but a bad tree bears bad fruit. It is not the service that we do but what character and conduct we display that shows if our hearts and minds have been transformed. I often turn to the scripture Galatians 5:22-23, But the fruit of the Spirit is love, joy, peace, forbearance, kindness, goodness, faithfulness, gentleness, and self-control. Against such things, there is no law. I pray that the Holy Spirit sheds light on the areas that I have not surrendered so that I can give them up and bear the fruits of the Spirit. Bearing this Fruit is not enough; it is just a starting point.

I must also walk in God's will for my life, but if we all focused on bearing the fruit of the Spirit, we would make an enormous impact on the world and lead more people to Christ. After all, letting go of the old us and becoming a new creation is for the glory of God to be manifested in our lives. It is beautiful to see when someone gets saved and lives a life full of God's purpose. We cannot get to this if we are still bound to the past. It is like an anchor keeping you from setting sail.

God desires for all of us to walk in freedom. Galatians 5:1 states that; It is for freedom that Christ has set us free; therefore, stand firm and do not let yourselves be burdened again by a yoke of slavery. Holding on to your past hurts or failures puts you into slavery to them. Stop carrying the yoke; it is not yours to bear. Jesus died for your sins so you could live free from bondage and experience a life with peace and joy. The minute I decided that it was time to let go, I surrendered. I started to see God move me from a place of no peace to a place full of peace and joy. Life can be lived in full abundance as we take on our new nature. If you knew that you were hindering your spiritual growth by holding on to your mask, would you take it off? He wants to rid you of all things that cause you to walk out of alignment. When we walk in alignment with God, we are deciding to trust him completely with our lives. We become dependent on Him to guide us. We must relinquish control and allow God to order our steps. Turning to God for direction in all things. It takes trust and faith to surrender it all to him.

Yielding to God's will involves accepting God's direction. It requires letting go of personal plans and desires. We must get to the understanding that He knows what is best and has plans for our lives. When I think back over my life, I would never have thought that God would have me marry a Pastor and live my life in church leadership. He knew the plan, and all it took was for me to give up some things and allow him to guide me. Many of us hold on to control because we do not understand his plan. Jeremiah 29:11 For I know the plans I have for you," declares the Lord, "plans to prosper you and not to harm you, plans to give you hope and a future. We cannot even begin to imagine all God has for us. In surrendering, we believe God knows what is best for us. We can go through our lives thinking that if we are in control, we can dictate the outcome. God is looking for vessels that can be molded so that he can get glory out of them. Surrendering to God's Will gives us the ability to walk in total alignment. As Jesus said, "Not my will, but your will be done."

Jesus surrendered to God's will and sacrificed himself so that we could be saved. What is God asking you to sacrifice? Surely, whatever it is, it will not bring death to you; if anything, it will cause you to soar to new heights in your spiritual walk with God. Getting to the point of wanting to let it go takes humility and submission. I had made up my mind that I would not date anymore. I came to the realization that I did not know how to choose my mate, and I only wanted who God had for me. I remember saying God, you are going to have to hit me over the head and tell me who my husband is. I was tired of the dating thing. I was now under the belief that the next Man God would bring, and I would date for the last time. I surrendered to God, knowing that he had the power to bring forth my husband in his timing. I felt content in my decision, and I waited patiently for God. The enemy, of course, sent men my way to tempt me. Each time this occurred, I remembered the covenant I made to God and did not give in. It was not long before my Husband was revealed to me. I am not saying that God's timing is quick; sometimes it takes a while.

Surrendering it over to God and allowing His will to come forth will always be your best choice. Relinquishing control and allowing God to lead. You mean you have learned that God's way is the only way for a Christian to live. When trials and tribulations come to you, knowing you are operating in God's will gives you the power to fight and be victorious.

Being centered in God's will gives you peace and confidence, knowing the battle is already won. I battled with depression for many years. I took medication and spent time in mental health facilities. Nothing seemed to work, and I was told I would never be free from depression. My Grandmother would often tell me that there is nothing God could do, and all that needed to be done was to pray. I prayed, and I heard God tell me that my condition was not what he had for me. I continue to pray, and I surrendered my depression to him, trusting that he would heal me. He began to heal my heart from the loss of my father, who was murdered by my stepmother when I was 6 years old. My grief has lasted most of my life. My unforgiveness towards my stepmother and my loss of my father were the root of my depression. It took time, but I am now free of depression. When it comes to our emotional healing, we need to know that God has already proclaimed victory! In Psalm 147:3, He heals the broken in heart and binds up their wounds.

It's time for your Next Chapter.

God wants you to surrender your hurt and pain to him. It is His will that you be made whole. Surrendering is an act of trust, obedience, and reliance on God's supernatural power. You cannot do it alone, but with God's will, all things are possible. I shared with you some of my biggest acts of surrender because these testimonies are evidence that we serve an awesome God who is waiting for you to let go. You may be asking God How do you let go of What they did to you.

The pain of the offense is real. You replay it in your mind, and it feels like it happened yesterday. Your heart stays hardened each time you think about it. Sis, God is asking for you to give it to him. He wants you to know that there is nothing you could ever go through that he has not already prepared a way out. Coming out of this freely will require you to forgive them. Jesus asks us to forgive so that we can learn to love like he does. He loves each one of us unconditionally. On the cross after being brutally beaten and ridiculed, he said to the father Forgive them, for they know not what they do. The act of compassion Jesus showed them is the same act of compassion we are to show to those who hurt us?

Forgiveness is for us to clean our hearts and to show the same love that was given to us when He died for our sins. The Bible tells us in Ephesians 4:32 Be kind to one another, tenderhearted, forgiving one another, as God in Christ forgave you. Forgiveness is a requirement to be forgiven. When we choose not to forgive, we cause ourselves so much harm. The enemy has a legal right to attack you.

Surrender It, Sis!

Many people have become sick in their bodies and minds because they chose to hold on to the offense. There is so much freedom waiting for you if you can just let it go. This thing has been keeping you angry and bitter for far too long. It has caused you to fall out of relationships that should never have been broken. This thing has caused you to close off a part of your heart that God is requiring you to give back to him. Each time I decided to let go and surrender my unforgiveness to God, I was released from strongholds that were destroying my life. God wants you to be healed and delivered. Your time is today, surrender your unforgiveness, Sis! Walking in freedom feels good. It took me years to understand this. Once I started letting go of things, I searched for more things that were holding me back. My grief was a stronghold that kept me in depression. God understood that we should grieve our loved ones. The Bible says in Matthew 5:4 Blessed are those who mourn, for they shall be comforted. Comfort is there for us if we surrender our grief to God. Many people believe that if I stop grieving, I will let go of my loved one. This is a misconception.

Your loved one would want you to be happy, free from grief, and living your life full and abundantly. If you lose someone tragically, it can take longer to come to terms with their passing. I can tell you that I felt my dad was taken from me too soon. I now understand that God decides the timing, and although I felt that I needed more time with Him, God does not make mistakes. He understands your pain, your loss, and your fears. He invites you to speak to him about your grief and heartache because he wants to accompany you on your grief journey. He desires to walk with you to

It's time for your Next Chapter.

uphold you and uplift you. The Bible says in 2 Corinthians 1: 3-4 Blessed be the God and Father of our Lord Jesus Christ, the Father of mercies and God of all comfort, who comforts us in all our affliction, so that we may be able to comfort those who are in any affliction, with the comfort with which we ourselves are comforted by God. We are to comfort each other during our grief journey with the comfort God gives. God uses grief to help us know him more, both as we receive His comfort and as our grief prompts us to more fully appreciate the gift of life and more deeply understand the reality of the effect of sins on the world. Grief connects us to God's heart. God understands our grief and offers to be with us, with promises from His word, and with the peace that passes all understanding Philippians 4:6-7. Death is always a season of grief for those left behind.

The Bible says in 1 Thessalonians 4: 13-14 But I do not want you to be ignorant brethren concerning those who have fallen asleep, lest you sorrow as others who have no hope. For if we believe that Jesus died and rose again, even so God will bring with him those who slept in Jesus. Paul reminds us to think of the death of a Christian as being asleep because it is a temporary state. Although we are sorrowful because we will not share any more earthly experiences with our departed Christian loved ones, we can also look forward to an eternity with them. The hope we have in Christ helps us to move forward through our grief. Sis, God is waiting for you to surrender your Grief to him. He wants to give you His comfort so that you can live with purpose in your heart. There is hope for all who are feeling down and depressed. It is important to know that if you are suffering from depression, it does not mean you do not love God or have faith. It means you are human, even some of the Bible's greatest servants experienced dark days. Overcoming depression is possible. The Bible says in Matthew 11: 28-30, Come to me all you who are weary and burdened, and I will give you rest. Take my yoke upon you, and learn from me, because I am humble in heart, and you will find rest for your souls, for my yoke is easy, and my burden is light. God knows your struggles and challenges, but He also never asked you to carry them by yourself. As you yield to Him and begin to trust that He will faithfully lead you every step of the way, you will begin to find more peace in your spirit. Even in the most difficult periods of my life when I felt depressed, I knew God was capable of healing me. It was the moment that I committed myself to getting to the root of my issues that I began to find the strength to fight back.

Sis, you have been suffering silently for too long. People tell you things will get better, but you have not convinced yourself that it will. You tend to focus on all the things going wrong and give little thought to the things that are going right. You have not found any joy in life and are simply going through the motions. Everything you set out to do seems to be a chore. There have been times when you wished your life would come to an end so you would not have to live another day in agony. God is waiting for you to allow him to deliver you from depression. The Bible says in Psalms 34: 17-19 The righteous cry out, and the Lord hears, and delivers them out of all their troubles. The Lord is near those who have a broken heart and saves such as have a contrite spirit. Many are the afflictions of the righteous, but the Lord delivers them out of them all. Sis, it is time you surrender depression to God. He has been waiting for you to get to the point is that you can no longer do this on your own.

He has been waiting for you to give it completely to him. The day will come when you will look back at this challenging time and realize the work God was doing behind the scenes. The Bible says in Psalms 3:3 But you, Lord, are my shield! You are my glory! You are the one who restores me. Depression can distort your thoughts, making you doubt yourself and everyone around you. The best thing you can do is trust in God, surrender, and let him fill you with His peace.

There are so many things God is waiting for you to line up to experience. The joy of marriage is one of God's gifts. To become one, you must have an open mind and the willingness to surrender to what is best for the two of you. Self-centeredness is a destroyer of a marriage. Many people take on the self-centered personality trait out of fear that they will not get their needs met. Otherwise, God did not give us the spirit of fear. So, we must surrender this to God so that we can let go of self-centeredness to become as one. As wives, we must also learn to submit. In our Christian Walk, we learn to submit to God. We trust God to be the head of our lives, allowing His will to become our will. In Marriage, we learn to submit to our Husbands. Trust must be established from the beginning. God has designed him to be the head and to lead the family according to his will. Knowing the vision and purpose for the marriage helps to establish the trust needed to submit. If you are dealing with emotional baggage from past relationships, this should be surrendered before getting married. Your husband deserves to have the absolute best of you. If you find yourself working through these things, and you're already married, this is the perfect time to surrender it to God. Marriage serves a Godly purpose, and people should be blessed by your marriage when they meet you. If God joined you together, it is not too late to make the changes necessary to have a healthy marriage. Let go of past mistakes. Forgive and create a clean slate with your spouse. Holding on to resentment keeps a wedge between you and your Husband.

Remember the vows you took and the way you loved each other from the beginning. Things can be even better than they were before. In marriage counseling, my husband and I encourage open and honest communication between couples. It is always surprising how the enemy attacks the communication. A lot of the time, the couples are seeing things from different perspectives. There are obvious signs of a breakdown in communication. We find that lots of resentment has settled in because of these different viewpoints. We help them to see where the miscommunication lies. If they are willing to make things work, the breakthrough is almost instant. Surrendering being right and being open to hearing how the other person feels goes far.

There is so much to fight for when you know God is in the midst. You must lay down your pride and come humbly seeking restoration. God will meet you in this place to open the lines of communication with your spouse. Resentment can be a subtle trick of the enemy. He uses this tactic to harden your heart towards your spouse. You get so caught up in your laundry list of all the things your spouse has failed to do. Often, you're so focused on what he is not doing, and you justify what you are not doing. It is time to see the enemy's scheme and to surrender your feelings of resentment to God. Sis, he is still the Man you loved, and he is still capable of making things work. You must put forth the effort and surrender all the disappointments, anger, and resentment.

Marriage does not have to be work. It was made by God to be a holy covenant. Mark 10:9 What therefore God hath joined together let not man put asunder. God is able to bring you two together stronger than before. It's not too late to start anew. Trust God and surrender it today! In a world filled with darkness, it is up to us to be the examples. Doing the work to release the old nature and take on the mind of Christ takes true commitment. We must discipline ourselves to achieve spiritual growth. For Christian's, without self-discipline, our appetites for comforts and pleasures can easily become our master and lead us into sin or otherwise hinder our spiritual walk. If the spiritual does not govern the physical, we can become easy targets of the enemy due to our lack of self-control.

The Bible says in Proverbs 25:28 A man without self-control is like a city broken into and left without walls. Self-control guides our decisions, and it correlates with how we show the other fruits of the Spirit in our lives. Displaying self-control is often a matter of responding rather than reacting. When we react to a situation, we let our emotions take control. We are more likely to become defensive and say hurtful things. As Christians, our responses to situations should be guided by the fruits of the Spirit. Sis, you have used your tongue as a weapon, cutting down people to defend yourself. Oftentimes, you go too far, saying words that are unforgettable. Each time you lash out, you feel sad about the things you have said and wish that you had held back. People know you as someone with a bad mouth, and people avoid confrontation with you. Your list of friends has gotten shorter because of your tongue. You burn bridges each time you get upset. If only you could take a second to think about what effect your words will have on the person you're lashing out at. Self-control does not come from self; it is a fruit of the Spirit.

The Holy Spirit provides us with the control we need when we surrender to him and spend time in his presence. The Bible says in Galatians 5:22, 24 But the fruit of the Spirit is love, joy, peace, patience, kindness, goodness, faithfulness, gentleness, self-control against such things, there is no law. And those who belong to Christ Jesus have crucified their flesh with its passions and desires. Sis, you can transform how you relate to people. God is waiting for you to surrender your hurt, anger, bitterness, and vindictiveness to him. Each time you lash out, you feel ashamed. That is the Holy Spirit convicting your heart. It is time to soften your heart and let your guard down. The enemy wants to isolate you and cause you to feel lonely and misunderstood. The enemy has tricked you into believing this is just the way you are. He has also tricked you into believing you will never have healthy relationships. It is time to let go of being right and wanting to have the last word. It is time to let go of wanting to hurt others because they hurt you. My husband often tells me you cannot control what others do, but you can control how you respond. Your light is meant to shine, Sis. You are a child of the true and living God. He wants you to be in fellowship with others. You were not made to stand alone. The Bible says in Hebrews 10: 24-25 And let us consider how we can spur one another on toward love and good deeds, not giving up meeting together, as some are in the habit of doing, but encouraging one another and all the more as you see the day approaching. Self-control is part of a Step-by-step process.

    The Bible says in 2 Peter 1: 5-7 But also for this very reason, giving all diligence, add to your faith virtue, to virtue knowledge, to knowledge self-control, to self-control perseverance, to perseverance godliness, to godliness brotherly kindness, and to brotherly kindness love. Through the act of surrendering prayer, the renewing of your mind, and accountability, you can obtain self-control. It is time to take back the relationships the enemy tried to destroy. It is time to be in the right fellowship with others, loving one another and building each other up instead of tearing them down. The victory is yours, Sis! There are so many things in our lives that we must surrender to live the way God intended, which is complete and abundant. There is vulnerability in letting go. When you have held on to a way of being for so long, there can be fear of what is to come once you let it go. Many people's fears are rooted in believing God is out to condemn them through their trials and hurts. This could be further from the truth because of Jesus' sacrifice. Through Jesus' sacrifice and resurrection, people now have a savior who took the punishment for their sins. This brings us to a place where God only wants to offer love, peace, and the opportunity to serve alongside Him.

There was a time when I was afraid to step out and do the work of the Lord. I was afraid that I would not give a word I received from God correctly. I was afraid my prayers for others in my intercession would not be answered. I was afraid to sing on the praise team. The enemy had me stuck in a holding place. I knew it was time to go forth, but I just did not know how. My husband shared his testimony on being shy and how God revealed to him that it was pride holding him back. I begin to realize that if God was sending me out, he was going to provide the anointing to carry out what I was sent to do. It was the fear of moving forward that kept me bound. Fears keep us bound from living up to our full potential. The Bible says in Isaiah 41:10 Fear not, for I am with you; be not dismayed, for I am God, I will strengthen you, I will help you, I will uphold you with my righteous hand. Remember, God is with you, and it is the Holy Spirit tugging on your heart to release these things that have been holding you back.

There is so much peace awaiting you. We do not need to fear tomorrow. God wants us to be filled with hope and trust, not fear. He has given us hope through the promise that he can uphold us by his strength today. Sis, God is calling you to a higher place in him. It is time you let go of the fear of walking in your true calling. The Bible says in Joshua 1:9 Have I not commanded you? Be strong and courageous. Do not be frightened, and do not be dismayed, for the Lord

It's time for your Next Chapter.

thy God is with you wherever you go. God will go before you and prepare the path; all you need to do is become a willing vessel. There is so much he has placed inside of you. Your testimonies of victories won! The gifting he wants to cultivate is all there. Do not let it lie dormant any longer. It is so rewarding to be used by God. We were all created to serve him, and your gifts and talents are needed. Do not let the enemy hold you back any longer. Do not sit on that word God told you to share. Do not be afraid to intercede for someone because we all have someone assigned to us. I had a dream that I was before the Lord on judgment day. He asked me about the souls I was to minister to. He gave an exact number. This astounded me, and I woke up realizing there is a precise number of people waiting for me to get into position and do the work of the Lord. The Bible says in Psalm 34:4 I sought the Lord, and He answered me and delivered me from all my fears. How reassuring it is to know that if you seek God, he will answer and deliver you from all of your fears. Once you get started, you look back at this pivoting moment and rejoice knowing that you have overcome the stronghold of fear. The Bible says in 2 Timothy 1:7 For God has not given us a spirit of fear, but of power, and of love, and of a sound mind. There is nothing too big for God, and he did not design you to live in fear. You are made to walk in power, to walk in love, and to walk with a sound mind.

Trust God today and surrender fear to Him, Sis. Those who are assigned to you are waiting for you to walk in your purpose. There has not been a time like this time in your life to move into the things of God. Deciding to let go of the things that have held you back takes courage. Our God can do all things. When you are at the point of surrendering, engaging in regular prayer and meditation on God's word can strengthen faith and help facilitate it. Prayer is agreeing with what God has already proclaimed. When we are in full agreement, that is when we see the power of our prayers being answered. You were never made to live a defeated life. God's plan was always to prosper you. Hearing God's voice, praying, and activating your faith will break any stronghold in your life. The Bible says in Mark 11:24 Therefore I tell you, whatever you ask in prayer, believe that you have received it, and it will be yours. What joy do we receive knowing God is a prayer-answering God? In my most trying times, I have seen the power of God move in my life and bring me to a place of victory. I look back at these moments, and I know without a shadow of doubt that through prayer, God delivered me. Each time this occurred, it strengthened my faith, for I personally know God will never forsake you.

    If you trust him with those hard things, the things you cannot seem to do on your own, you will see for yourself just how capable he is of delivering you out of them. There are too many of us saints sharing our testimonies for us to be wrong. You have to approach surrendering with a humble spirit. The Bible says in 1 Peter 5:5-6 likewise you younger people, submit yourself to your elders. Yes, all of you be submissive to one another, and be clothed in humility for God resists the proud but gives grace to the humble. Therefore, humble yourselves under the mighty hand of God, that he may exalt you over time. If we exalt ourselves, we place ourselves in opposition to God's will. But if we humble ourselves, God gives us more grace and exalts us. God is looking to exalt you over your strongholds. A breakthrough comes when we submit, knowing only God can deliver us. Humility is not an easy virtue to exercise. It takes courage, discipline, and faith to put humility into daily practice. We are to have fear of the Lord. Not the type of fear of being scared, but a fear of knowing he is all-powerful. It acknowledges that God deserves all the glory and honor. Being humble means we are wholly dependent on God, knowing we are nothing without him. The Bible says in James 4:10 Humble yourself in the sight of the Lord and He will lift you up. Sis, God is about to exceed your expectations. He has been waiting for you to come to this place of humility and submission. It is in this moment that you can truly see a powerful move of God on your behalf. Along with being humble and submitting, you also need to trust and have faith. Trusting is not exactly the same as faith, which is a gift from God. Trusting is believing in the promises of God in all circumstances, even when evidence seems to point out something different. The Bible says in Proverbs 3:5 Trust in the Lord with all thy heart and lean not to your own understanding. The things you have gone through have been very difficult. Yet it had a purpose. God's purpose for our trials and tribulations is to grow us spiritually. When we experience things and turn to him, He is able to show us how much He loves us by delivering us out of our circumstances. If you have never gone through anything, how could you confess how faithful God is? Sis, it is time to change your perspective.

    We want the blessings and the anointing, but we don't want the trials that bring forth the blessings and the anointing. There is no quick and painless path. We all have to go through something in order to gain something. Our trust in God is proven through our faith to hold on to the word he has spoken over our lives. When we surrender those things to God, we give him the ability to change the direction our lives are heading. We come from a path the enemy has laid out for us into full alignment with His purpose and plan for us. Through this, we go through healing and deliverance. The Bible says in 1 Peter 5:10 But may the God of all grace, who has called us to his external glory by Jesus Christ, after you have suffered for a while, perfect, establish, strengthen, and settle you.

It is God's plan to make you whole and complete in Him. You must trust the process, knowing you will come out better than you ever imagined you would. One of my favorite verses from the song The Refiner goes like this. I want to be tried by fire, purified, you take whatever you desire, Lord, here's my life. That is exactly what God wants from us. He is waiting for us to give him our lives and to want us to go through whatever it is takes to be purified. Sis, giving up those things that have been holding you down may seem hard, but it is the sort of sacrifice that will reap rewards. You must have faith that he will do the very things He has promised you. The righteous are never forsaken. Letting go of control of what you may have thought the outcome should be and allowing God's will to come forth is what true surrender looks like. Many of us let our own anxieties and doubts get in the way, and we feel the need to take over. We sit our faith down, and in reality, we take back what we gave to God. That is like playing a yo-yo with God. We must trust God and surrender it to him and let go of control of it. God cannot do the miraculous if we are trying to be in control. God does not need our help. We do not even know what the outcome of deliverance truly looks like unto we go through it.

There were times in my own life when I said I was giving something to God and found myself still pondering over it. I had to ask myself why I was still worrying about this thing when I had already told God I could not handle it, and I was giving it over to him. I discovered that I was not walking in faith, and I was becoming impatient with God. I wanted control of the outcome of the situation. I quickly realized that I was slowing down the process by stepping in. We sabotage ourselves when we get in God's way. We need to fully surrender those things to Him and be still. The enemy will make you believe that God is not going to deliver you. He will cause you to feel impatient in the process. The Bible says in Isaiah 30:18 Therefore, the Lord will wait, that He may be gracious to you; and therefore He will be exalted, that He may have mercy on you. For the Lord is a God of justice; blessed are all those who wait for Him.

Sis, be patient in your surrendering and deliverance process. God's timing is perfect and always on time. By waiting patiently, you are building your faith and also pleasing God. Let go of the control and let God have his way in your life. All he is looking for is your yes and amen. The rest He has in His hands. Expressing praise and worship to God can deepen surrender. When we choose to worship in faith, despite our feelings, God sets in motion things only seen in the spiritual realm. What goes on in the spiritual realm will eventually show up in the natural.

God is looking for those hearts that can worship him through any circumstance. When we praise and worship, it takes our minds off the issue and places our focus on God. The Bible says in Isaiah 26:3 You will give him perfect peace whose mind stays on you. You deepen your surrender when you choose to focus on God instead of what you have given to him. It is an act of faith. If we choose praise and worship over doubt and fear, we will find ourselves living in peace and not easily swayed by our trials and tribulations.

We were created to be in worship of God at all times. His word tells us to cast all of our cares on him. He wants us to live our lives with the peace of God that surpasses all understanding. Giving your burdens to Him and letting them go is what we are required to do. In writing this book, I realize just how many things are designed to keep us from living life full and abundantly. It was never the plan for us. We have an enemy that wants to keep us from praising and worshiping our God. If he can keep you distracted with all of those things that keep you bound, then he can keep you from experiencing the joy of serving the Lord. I do not take lightly all the battles God has won on my behalf. Each time I got to the point where I realized this was not my battle to fight and gave it to the Lord, it got easier to just let it all go. I now choose to make surrendering a daily act. I no longer want to become stagnant. I want to walk in new realms and dimensions with the Lord. Sis, you have made a new commitment to God to not allow yourself to be in bondage. You have surrendered those things that have not served your purpose. Now you can walk in total freedom. It's time to hold your head up high and rejoice in knowing that with God, you can conquer anything. You are a warrior, and with each victory, you have gained wisdom on how to defeat the adversary. Your weapons have been sharpened, and you know personally how to use them for the next battle. You walk into each battle focused on how you will see God move.

    Instead of worrying about the battle, you'll get excited. Now that you're walking in this place, it is time you reach out to help another sister who is struggling with surrendering. We are all a part of the body of Christ, and we need to function as a whole. Sharing our testimonies of how we overcame the enemy helps others draw the faith needed to win their battles. As we overcome, we grow stronger together. How powerful would we be if we all made it our purpose to reach out and help another sister? We would see many free and walking in victory. Now is the time to take what you have known and use it for good. We can teach others how to take off the mask and receive healing and deliverance. We can teach each other how to surrender completely to God. We do not have to hold back. We can push forward in total transparency. Knowing what we share with our sisters encourages them to stand against the enemy and believe that with God, the battle is already won.

Surrender It, Sis!

It's time for your Next Chapter.

Co-Author
Sis. Tisha M. Clay,
(M.S., Ed. Special Education)
(M.A. Ed. Educational Counseling)

Seven Days of Prayer that Will Change Your Life

Surrendering is something we all struggle with as women. Letting go of our past hurts allows us to heal and walk into all that GOD has for us. Growing up, I experienced a lot of pain and rejection starting at the age of eight. I knew of GOD but didn't truly know HIM. I felt that since HE didn't know me, HE wasn't obligated to save or help me, and wondered why He would want to. GOD had a special plan arranged for my life, and HIS timing was perfect. In my early twenties, something began to stir in my spirit. I was two years away from moving out of my mother's house and ready to stand on my own.

Surrender It, Sis!

GOD knew that was the perfect time for HIM to get a hold of me. In my junior year of college, the young man I was dating fell sick and ended up in the hospital on life support. I remember sitting alone in the family waiting room at the hospital, crying out to GOD. I prayed that if HE spared this young man's life, I would give my life to HIM. Only GOD and I knew about that prayer. Of course, when you pray to GOD and put HIM on the spot, HE will test you to see if you are going to be a woman of your word.

Quick note: Be careful what you pray for, because sure enough, the next morning, GOD healed that young man, and he woke up. It was at that point that I knew I had to break up with this young man and give my life to Christ. It was tough and heartbreaking to end that relationship, but I had to stay true to my word. I ended the relationship, gave my life to Christ, and joined my co-worker's church. I remember thinking, okay, Lord, I am saved now, what should I do next?

GOD showed me I needed to find out who HE is. The things that I used to hear about GOD were so contrary to HIS word. One thing I used to hear often was that HE was a mean man who invoked fear because look at all of the crime in this world. What loving GOD would allow all of this crime to happen on a daily basis? I also heard that HE put diseases on you so you would come to HIM so HE could heal you. After seeking HIM and reading HIS word for myself, I quickly learned none of those things were true. Now I know why HE wanted me to find out who HE was for myself. GOD is a loving father who created this world so that we would know

HIM as a provider. A provider that will never leave HIS family. Hebrews 13:5 KJV states, "I will never leave thee, nor forsake thee". HE provides love, peace, joy, comfort, help, and support. It is all a free gift included in our salvation; the Hebrew and Greek words for salvation imply the ideas of deliverance, safety, preservation, healing, and soundness (Schofield Study Bible, 1909 reference edition). Exodus 15:2 states, "The Lord is my strength and song, and he is become my salvation: he is my God". GOD is our source of strength; everything we need in this life comes from HIM. In HIM we are safe, saved, healed, and prosperous. Outside of HIM, we have none of these things. HE will give us guidance and direction once we commit our lives to HIM. Regardless of what we do or how far we stray away, HE will always be there to receive us with open arms. There is a parable in the Bible, in the book of Luke, chapter 15, that tells the story of the prodigal son. The father was overjoyed when his son returned home after he had strayed away. That is precisely how GOD feels about us.

There were many times after I gave my life to Christ that I would purposely not attend church. I can laugh about it now, but my pastor would call me the prodigal daughter. Sometimes it just felt better to sit at home and isolate. I was so used to being alone that being in a small family church where everyone is concerned about you and loving on you was a lot. I was so young, sad, and broken that I did not want to impose any of my sadness on them, so I stayed at home. I think I cried the most after I got saved because, for the longest time, I held all my emotions inside. I grew up thinking crying was a sign of weakness, not realizing it was a release that needed to happen for God to heal my brokenness. It was also part of my salvation, Psalm 51:10 states, "Create in me a clean heart, O God; and renew a right spirit within me". My views of life were more negative than positive. I used to question if I even deserved anything good in life. This was mainly because I had my son when I was a teenager, so the shame of being a teen mom made me feel like a hard life was my consequence. Once I gave my life to Christ and truly surrendered all to HIM, HE opened so many doors for me. God made a way when there was no way for job opportunities, college admissions, and financial independence. I am a firm believer in GOD and HIS word, especially the scripture Ephesians 3:20KJV, "Now unto him that is able to do exceedingly abundantly above all that we ask or think, according to the power that worketh in us". The blessing overflow can only happen through our salvation and commitment to HIM.

    I was not committed to HIM the way I should have been in the early stages of my relationship with HIM. The reason being I was afraid I was going to have a boring life serving HIM. Once again, my distorted way of thinking mainly came from hearing about other people's opinions and thoughts about being a Christian. When I look back, I spoke with some very unhappy people who were struggling in their Christian Walk. You must know GOD for yourself and seek HIM daily. Matthew 6:33 states, "But seek ye first the kingdom of GOD, and HIS righteousness; and all these things shall be added unto you". You must seek HIM to let go of your worldly thoughts and worldly ways. Hence, why I refer to it as my distorted way of thinking, these worldly thoughts and ways were with me all this time before I gave my life to Christ. Just as I had to surrender my distorted way of thinking, you too will have to surrender it all and let it go. It will not be an easy process because the enemy does not want you to let go of your worldly thoughts and worldly ways. That is how he can keep you in bondage, running away from Christ.

When I asked GOD for spiritual guidance, HE blessed me with spiritual parents, my pastor John H. Clark and his wife, Norma Clark. I remember one of the first things my pastor told me was renew your mind and he gave me the scripture Romans 12:2, "And be not conformed to this world: but be ye transformed by the renewing of your mind, that ye may prove what is that good, and acceptable, and perfect, will of God". My next question was How do I renew my mind? Pastor said, "You have to change your speech," and he gave me the scripture Proverbs 18:21, "Death and life are in the power of your tongue". As a baby Christian, I would pray to GOD and tell him all my problems, then take the issues back and speak negative things out of frustration over the prayer that I had just prayed. Then I would wonder why my situation was not changing. I was focusing on my problems and not on GOD. God's word says in 1 Peter 5:7, "Casting all your care upon him; for he careth for you." It's such a hard thing for us to do, to let go of that tug of war. The tug-of-war in which we cast all our cares on God and then take them right back. Which means HE cannot do anything when we take it back from HIM, we are supposed to give it to HIM and trust HIM with it.

Surrender It, Sis!

Being newly saved was a lot to take part in, GOD knew that. HE gave me the idea of how seven days of prayer could change my perspective, life, and faith walk with HIM. Every day of the week became a specific prayer day for the issues and concerns that were weighing me down. Marriage Monday, Trustful Tuesday, Worry Free/Worship Wednesday, Thankful Thursday, Faith-filled Friends and Family Friday, Self-Saturday, and Submission Sunday. Praying every day about specific areas in my life helps me to strengthen my relationship with GOD.

Marriage Monday

Marriage Monday was the day when I prayed fervently for my married friends, my future husband, my single friends, and my divorced friends. I did not grow up with a good example of what a healthy, godly marriage looks like. The ideas of a healthy marriage that I saw came from television and books that I read, which obviously are not reality. When I gave my life to Christ, I didn't think marriage was in my future. But after I got saved, GOD had me study on what a godly wife looks like. The first scripture HE gave me was 1 Corinthians 7:34, "But she, that is married, careth for the things of this world, how she may please her husband." God began to show me that I needed to prepare to be a godly wife, just like when you get trained for a new job. To be the godly wife that GOD desired for you to be I had to know what the godly wife expectations were. What I first learned was that to be a godly wife requires you extending your husband an unlimited amount of grace.

God gives us grace; that same grace needs to be extended to your husband. The main reason is that he is going to make mistakes and possibly disappoint you. You have to know how to respond to him; everything is about presentation. An example would be my spiritual parents don't argue. I remember thinking, why not? There is no way that they agree on everything all of the time. I grew up in a house where my parents argued a lot, which instilled so much fear in me about healthy relationships. My spiritual parents didn't argue because Mrs. Clark chose her responses carefully. She sought GOD in everything, especially in her reactions to her husband. Mrs. Clark told me one day he couldn't argue with himself, and if I hold my tongue, then he will stop. This is why they never argued; I don't know what she was thinking when he was fussing. Job 29:10KJV states, "The nobles held their peace, and their tongue cleaved to the roof of their mouth". She is a truly noble woman, and just because she didn't respond does not mean she always agreed.

What I learned from the bible is it's okay, to agree to disagree the scripture says in Philippians 2:14 Do all things without murmurings and disputings:" At the end of the day, you don't want anything to come between you and your husband, you don't want to give the enemy anything to cause division in your marriage. Remember, you are to be your husband's biggest cheerleader on the sidelines. You want to build him up, not tear him down. No one can pray for your husband like you can, not his mother, siblings, or even his children. A wife knows her husband in a role that no one else knows. Your husband should be your best friend. Oftentimes, we women know exactly what to do to upset him. But many times we don't know what to do to please him and make him happy. What are his hobbies, music and movie genres, what sports and food does he like? If he is truly your best friend, you need to know these things about him. The man that GOD has for you, you will complement each other. He will be strong in the areas where you are weak; you will be strong in the areas where he is weak. Your marriage will be a testament and a ministry that GOD will use in a mighty way for his kingdom.

As a single woman, we are to be single and serving the Lord 1 Corinthians 7:34 states, but he that is unmarried careth for the things of the Lord, how he may please the Lord". Now, what serving looks like to you is going to be different for everyone. It could be serving in your church, your community, at work, or in your family. Only you and God know the call that He has on your life and the ministries He wants to evolve through you. I realize that not all single women desire to be married, but this scripture still pertains to you. Whether you have been called to a life of singleness or want to be married, you still have to know what pleases GOD. The only way to know what pleases HIM is to strengthen your relationship with HIM. How you improve your relationship is by reading HIS word and attending church regularly. Hebrews 10:25 states, "Not forsaking the assembling of ourselves together, as the manner of some is; but exhorting one another: and so much the more, as ye see the day approaching". It is very easy to isolate yourself as a single woman, but when we do that, the enemy can slowly pull us away from GOD, as the enemy knows there is

It's time for your Next Chapter.

strength in numbers.

When starting a new job, the company requires you to attend an orientation. Being single is a way of life that prepares you to be a godly wife. With divorce rates being the way that they are, single women need to know how to be a godly wife, which is very different than a worldly wife. Being truly prepared for marriage is a sure way to avoid being a part of the divorce statistics. Preparing for marriage will help you understand the importance of having a spiritual foundation.

GOD and HIS word have to be that spiritual foundation, when you two become one HE is the only other person in your marriage, "And if one prevail against him, two shall withstand him; and a threefold cord is not quickly broken", Ecclesiastes 4:12KJV. Every day, you and your husband have to make a conscious effort to show up for one another in the little things and the big things. If you don't know that or prepare for that, you are giving the enemy free range in your marriage. Which means it is very likely that your marriage will fail and end in divorce. GOD did not call us women to fail at marriage, especially once we know the truth and are prepared. Now you can't make your partner put in the work, but if you allow GOD to bring you the man that HE has for you, your husband will willingly put in the work. Because he will know you as his help meet, Genesis 2:18 KJV, "And the Lord God said, It is not good that the man should be alone; I will make him an help meet for him", and a blessing from GOD Proverbs 18:22, "Whoso findeth a wife findeth a good thing and obtaineth favor of the Lord."

Surrender It, Sis!

Since I am not married yet, I do not know the emotional toll of divorce. I only know the emotional toll of being a child in a divorced home. My parents separated when I was eight years old and divorced years later. That hurt and pain that I felt as a child was very hard, my whole world felt like it was shattered. As an adult, the pain of losing your spouse and family must be excruciating, especially if there was infidelity from one of the spouses. I can remember one instance where one of my girlfriends answered her husband's phone and there was a young woman on the other end telling her that her husband was cheating and they thought she ought to know. I remember her calling me screaming on the phone. I thought someone in her family had died. She was crying hysterically because her husband had just confessed everything to her about his infidelity. She didn't know what to do, and I remember supporting her through her phases of grief with her marriage. She blamed herself for her failing marriage. I reminded her that three people were supposed to be in that marriage: her husband, herself, and GOD. I would let her vent and guide her to GOD and HIS word. I would tell her to let GOD heal her broken heart, "Psalm 34:18 KJV, The Lord is nigh unto them that are of a broken heart; and saveth such as be of a contrite spirit". I would also tell her to let GOD deal with her husband. It was not her place to do things on purpose to hurt him because she was hurting. GOD was the only one who knew her actual pain and could guide and direct her on her next steps.

Trustful Tuesday

It's time for your Next Chapter.

The dictionary defines trust as, "firm belief in the reliability, truth, ability, or strength of someone or something". When I look at this definition, there is a lot to unpack. A firm belief means you cannot be swayed; you have to stand firm in whatever you are trusting GOD for. Due to my trust issues, it made it hard to trust GOD, at least that's what I thought when I first got saved. Giving God my heart was hard because I was afraid He would break it too. I invoked all my past hurts onto HIM. I even wondered if HE would hurt me too, not realizing that hurting me was against who HE is. Growing up, I was very naive in thinking that everyone could be trusted, I would put my faith and trust in people and not GOD. I always wanted to believe that people had good intentions for me. I felt like if I showed you that I am a woman of my word, then you should do the same. Many times, that was not the case; I was rejected, betrayed, and heartbroken. I was left with confusion and hurt feelings. I could not understand how people could be so cruel. That is how Trustful Tuesday came into fruition.

Trusting God with my broken heart meant giving it to him so he could heal all of my past hurts. I needed to be free from my trust issues so that I could move into HIS plan for my life. I asked GOD to give me a discerning spirit and whom to let in my inner circle, to avoid unnecessary heartbreak. Psalm 62:8KJV, "Trust in him at all times; ye people, pour out your heart before him: God is a refuge for us, Selah". I needed to pour out everything in my heart and not hold back in fear. GOD became my comforter and confidant as John 14:16KJV states, "And I will pray the Father, and he shall give you another Comforter, that he may abide with you forever". I would vent and talk to GOD like he was sitting next to me on my couch. My heart was overwhelmed with hurt because I had experienced so much emotional trauma at such a young age. Once I poured everything out, GOD then showed me that I had to learn to trust people again. I remember thinking I don't want to feel all the hurt and pain that I felt before when interacting with people. I would purposely shy away and withdraw from people any time I saw a glimpse of them trying to hurt me. This is how I deciphered when I was leaning on my own understanding. My perception of trust was to trust no one because they would only hurt you. GOD's way is to trust ME, as I am the only one who will not hurt you. God reminded me that I needed to trust Him because He knew the bigger picture. Proverbs 3:5-6 KJV states, "Trust in the Lord with all thine heart; and lean not unto thine own understanding. In all thy ways acknowledge him, and he shall direct thy paths". My church family was my first test, allowing them to love on me, help, and support me was a huge blessing. Now, if I had not been obedient to GOD and let my church family into my heart, I would not be the healed woman of GOD that I am today. The women in my church were very instrumental in shaping me into becoming a strong and resilient woman of GOD.

    Trusting GOD in those hard transitional times in life is rough. Many times, I would ask GOD, Can you just come down and sit with me on the couch and explain to me why my friends, family, and I had to go through these hurtful trials and tribulations. Trusting GOD with guiding your life when you need a new job, home, car, or guidance with your finances goes against worldly views. The world's view is I need to talk with several people and get their perspectives on the decisions I need to make. GOD's way, which is, Psalm 34:7KJV, "BE still and know that I am GOD". Waiting for GOD to give you guidance and direction is part of being still. We cannot lean on our own understanding; we have to know and understand that HE knows the beginning from the ending. We have to be cautious, especially when there's another person involved, because you don't know what that person is thinking. You don't understand why they made those decisions. Trusting God requires faith, faith in what you cannot see and in what you do not understand. GOD's word says, "2 Corinthians 5:7, "For we walk by faith, not by sight". I did not know how I was going to be able to walk by faith all of the time and not be bogged down with the weight of worry. Worrying if GOD was going to lead me the right way as I continued to trust in HIM.

Worry Free Wednesday

How else can we lift our burdens? Worshiping GOD with Gospel and Christian music was such a blessing to me. Music was an integral part of my childhood, and secular music was always playing in my house or the car. I love to listen to the lyrics of music. Words are so powerful, and I did not realize that until I came to Christ. Growing up, I was a worrywart; I was even voted most worrisome in high school. I wanted to change that narrative so bad. When I looked up worry in the bible, I was first brought to Matthew 6:25-26KJV," Therefore I say unto you, Take no thought for your

Surrender It, Sis!

life, what ye shall eat, or what ye shall drink; nor yet for your body, what ye shall put on. Is life not more than meat, and the body than raiment? Behold the fowls of the air: for they sow not, neither do they reap, nor gather into barns; yet your heavenly Father feedeth them. Are ye not much better than they?". Worrying is not good for your body or your overall health; it wreaks havoc on women's hormones, your heart, and digestive system. I worried because I cared too much about people and their thoughts and beliefs, rather than focusing on myself. I love the reference about birds in that scripture. Birds get up every morning, singing loudly at our windows, and fly all around us daily. One thing birds don't do is worry; they are a true testament of what it means to trust GOD. They trust GOD to guide them where to get food and where the puddles of water are for them to drink and take a bath. They have no cares in this world because they know GOD always provides. I like to call that bird faith, I need some of that sometimes in my life, do you?

Have you ever sat and watched a bird play in a puddle of water? One day while I was at work, there was a big puddle of water near my classroom door, because it had rain the night before. A little bird flew down out of nowhere and started playing, singing, and splashing in that water. As I was watching this bird, I thought to myself, that bird woke up this morning and was like Lord, I am hungry, thirsty, and I need to take a bath. GOD guided and directed that bird to that puddle of water. Now had that bird not been obedient and listened to GOD, it would have never had its heart's desires fulfilled. I laugh to myself every time I think about how that bird was playing and singing in that puddle of water, without a care in this world. I believe that is how worry-free GOD wants us to be. If HE can provide for those birds, we have to trust and believe that HE can and will do the same for HIS children. Worry-free worship is like that bird playing and singing in that puddle of water. We have to worship GOD, knowing that HE can and will do what HE says HE will do. Isaiah 55:11 states KJV, "So shall my word be that goeth forth out of my mouth: it shall not return unto me void, but it shall accomplish that which I please, and it shall prosper in the thing whereto I sent it".

God loves to remind me where HE has brought me from. Especially during praise and worship, I tend to get very emotional just thinking about my past before Christ. I may not be exactly where I want to be, but I am not back there, where I used to be. GOD has blessed me with so much, and I know HE's not done.

Music has always been a coping tool for me, whether I was happy, sad, mad, or whatever emotion I was feeling. But when I got saved, gospel and Christian music hit differently, because the words would minister to my heart, and lift my spirits. I miss going into a Christian bookstore. I could be in there for hours, looking at different books. I would always end up at the music section before I left the store. They used to have the little five-dollar CD section, my very first five-dollar CD was Fred Hammond. I listened to that "Pages of Life Chapters I & II" CD so much, and I would tell everybody to go and get it. The lyrics in those songs were helpful in getting me through that season of life that I was currently in. The lyrics ministered to my heart because they were always how I was feeling at the time. Gospel and Christian music helped me get through a lot of sleepless nights. I would be up singing and praising GOD all hours of the night sometimes. There is something about worship when you are feeling down. It can instantly lift your spirits. Crying and singing were my therapy when I first got saved, and still are to this day. Listening and singing those music lyrics would give me hope that, although my present circumstances were overwhelming. It was not my end. GOD still had many things planned for me and my life. Worship reminds us of how good GOD is in the present and how good HE has been in the past. HE is truly worthy of all of our praise. Can I challenge to praise GOD one day like nobody is watching?

Thankful Thursday

"Thankful Thursday" was my way of thanking GOD in advance and not asking him for anything. Reverencing HIM for all that he has done for me and all that HE has yet to do. I don't think I truly understood what that phrase meant until I got saved, that says, "If HE doesn't do anything else HE's done enough". After I read Jesus' story in the Bible, how can we not thank HIM? John 3:16 KJV states, "For God so loved the world, that he gave his only begotten Son, that whosoever believeth in him should not perish, but have everlasting life." GOD sent his only son to die on that cross for every past, present and future sin that we could ever commit, is more than enough for us to thank HIM daily. There's another phrase that states ten thousand tongues could never thank HIM enough, and that is so true. All of the extra blessings that HE does just because. It's a blessing when I cry out and HE shows up every time. I love Psalm 34:17 KJV, which states, "The righteous cry, and the Lord heareth, and delivereth them out of all their troubles". HE truly does not have to do any of the things we ask for. But because of HIS love for us, HE does it. When I think about the favor on my job and the healing and the grace that I didn't deserve, HE asks nothing in return but my obedience, and that is sometimes too hard. Yet HE will still bless anyway, it's one of the many reasons why we need to thank HIM fervently. If we can fervently pray to HIM and ask him for things, then we can fervently thank and praise HIM. How many times in a day can we honestly say that we thank GOD? I know I'm guilty, it is usually a few times during the day, but nowhere near where it should be, which is so sad because HE deserves it and HE doesn't even require it.

Paul states in 1Corinthians KJV 15:1-4, "Moreover, brethren, I declare unto you the gospel which I preached unto you, which also ye have received, and wherein ye stand; By which also ye are saved if ye keep in memory what I preached unto you, unless ye have believed in vain. For I delivered unto you first of all that which I also received, how that Christ died for our sins according to the scriptures; And that he was buried, and that he rose again the third day according to the scriptures". Once again here is another reminder about our salvation through Jesus Christ, what HE has done for us and all of the free benefits that we receive daily. There should never be a day where we are not Thanking GOD for sending our big brother JESUS to die on that cross and save us from a horrible life of sin and death. My challenge to you is to place a Thank You Jesus post-it on your bathroom mirror or somewhere you know you will see it daily. Every day let's start blessing HIM with the reverence that HE deserves.

Faith-filled Friends and Family Friday

What exactly is Faith, GOD's word states in the Amplified bible, "Now faith is the assurance (title deed, confirmation) of things hoped for (divinely guaranteed), and the evidence of things not seen [the conviction of their reality—faith comprehends as fact what cannot be experienced by the physical senses]". Whatever we are praying for, we have to believe that it is going to happen, and that goes completely against our five senses. An example of this is how do we know we are truly saved? After reading the plan of salvation in Romans 10:9-10KJV, "That if thou shalt confess with thy mouth the Lord Jesus, and shalt believe in thine heart that God hath raised him from the dead, thou shalt be saved. For with the heart, man believeth unto righteousness; and with the mouth confession is made unto salvation". The scripture is clear, there is no possession to be saved without confessing it first. Once we do that, then we are saved through faith.

Our faith actually starts in that moment, and we continue to believe in faith that we are saved as one of GOD's daughters. Believe it or not, but it takes the same amount of faith to be saved as it does to believe God for any and everything else that we need. Also remember GOD's word states in Matthew 17:20, "And Jesus said unto them, Because of your unbelief: for verily I say unto you, If ye have faith as a grain of mustard seed, ye shall say unto this mountain, Remove hence to yonder place; and it shall remove; and nothing shall be impossible unto you". Have you ever seen a mustard seed? It's actually very tiny, one to two millimeters to be exact, but it can grow as tall as twenty to thirty feet, and its branches and leaves can span out another twenty feet wide. That is a very small amount of faith that we need to have for us to see blessings unfold in our lives. Can I challenge you again to believe GOD for the unimaginable with your mustard seed of faith?

Friends and Family Friday came about because I am one of those people who, if I tell you I'm going to pray for you, I want to honor my word. My Intercessory prayer time is every Friday. There were many people around me who would ask me to pray for them. Sometimes I would forget, and then I would feel bad if I heard a not-so-good update about someone who asked for prayer. I have learned that as a busy woman, I need to write things down so I don't forget. I used a prayer journal to write my friends and family members' names down to make sure I remembered their prayer requests. I also wanted whoever asked me for prayer to see that GOD's people can be trusted to do HIS work. Proverbs 17:17 states, "A friend loveth at all times". GOD encourages us to support and help one another. The bible also states in Acts 20:35, "I have shewed you all things, how that so labouring ye ought to support the weak". We need to do better in supporting our brothers and sisters in Christ. There are many other worldly organizations that band together and support each other. Should be the example, and yet many of those organizations are setting an example for us. The sad thing about that is those organizations know the truth about there being strength in numbers. We need to realize as Christians that joining together will help us to see more answered prayers. GOD loves it when we come together as a family as one strong unit.

GOD has blessed me with the gift to encourage people. I love to encourage people to trust GOD and try HIM so they can see how faithful HE is. I would buy little encouragement cards, business size, and pass them out to anyone and everyone. Because they had scriptures, people would always ask me, "How did you know that I needed that?" I would always respond I didn't, that was a message sent from GOD; I was just HIS vessel getting that information to you. GOD always knew who to send me to, when I would encourage people, I would also be encouraging myself. When we need guidance or need encouragement, all we have to do is ask, and GOD will send us someone to encourage, pray, and minister to our spirits. Many of my friends and family members just needed someone to listen to them and give them words of hope. That is a free gift that we can give to our brothers and sisters in Christ who might just need a little pick-me-up. Can I challenge you to ask GOD how you can encourage someone in your life today? Let HIM lead you to the person or people HE would like for you to encourage. He will also tell you exactly how you can do it. Remember, your return gift is coming from GOD, not from whoever you encourage. You will be surprised by how good you feel after you encourage someone.

It's time for your Next Chapter.

Self-Saturday

Society has told us for years that when we focus on ourselves, we are being selfish. But the reality is that most of us women are caregivers; we are caring for husbands, boyfriends, children, parents, siblings, and animals. That is just in our home, and that is not including our jobs. I called my Saturdays Self-Care Saturday, even though it should be Selfish Saturday. That was the day that I told myself that I needed to do something for myself. Now granted, some of us cannot give one full day to ourselves, maybe we can only do an hour or two. It just has to be something that you do for yourself and your mental health. Many times, we take on so many roles that we forget who we are. Self-Saturday will remind you that you need to take care of yourself so you can still help others. Pouring into yourself needs to be a requirement, just like you pour into others, because you matter too.

Since I became a mother at such a young age, my identity was only mom, so by the time my son became a teenager, he no longer wanted to hang out with me. My feelings were SO hurt because I had made him my world, and it took me years to figure out who exactly I was. I am still on that self-discovery journey. It was not until after taking many counseling courses to obtain my educational counseling master's degree that I realized the importance of self-care. I like to use the example on the airplane when the oxygen mask comes down, you are supposed to give yourself the oxygen first and then to your child. I used to think that was such a horrible thing, like how could someone do that? In actuality, if you give the oxygen to your child first, and something happens to you. Who's going to take care of your child?

Praying for myself and my needs on Self-Saturday is my priority. It took me a lot of years to learn to pray for myself like I did for other people. My caregiver and serving spirit can be very hard to put down. I consistently pour out and don't have enough energy or time to refill. My Self- Saturday has been evolving since I gave my life to Christ. In the beginning, it was me reading one of my favorite books. When I first got saved, I found this book at the Christian bookstore, and it was called "Prayers and Promises for Teens". That was a very powerful little book. There was a scripture for every emotion and situation that you could be facing. I would sit and read that book for hours over and over and over again. I couldn't completely understand at first why I kept reading that book. It truly helped me to deal with a lot of spiritual battles that I was facing.

God's word states, " Thy word is a lamp unto my feet, and a light unto my path". I needed to strengthen my shield of faith to combat all the enemy's fiery darts that he was shooting towards me. Ephesians 6:16 states, "Above all, taking the shield of faith, wherewith ye shall be able to quench all the fiery darts of the wicked". I began to deal with certain areas in my life that I knew needed a lot of spiritual guidance. Combating fear was a big issue that I really needed help with on Self-Saturday. I allowed fear to hold me back from doing so many things in life. I was scared to travel, venture out, and try new things, or even talk to people before I gave my life to Christ. Many things contributed to this, but I believe a major contributor was my distorted way of thinking. I would think that something bad was going to happen if I traveled somewhere out of my normal routine. Venturing out and trying something new was terrifying. There were so many negative thoughts going through my mind. I was not refilling the thoughts in my mind with anything positive. I would even think that if you said something positive, the outcome would be negative, and if you said something negative, the outcome would be positive. This distorted view of thinking is so contrary to GOD's word, Proverbs 18:21 states, " Death and life are in the power of the tongue". I had to quickly get out of the negative and into the positive, as I was stopping my own blessings over my life, with what I was thinking and praying.

    Sometimes we women talk ourselves out of so many wonderful experiences due to fear. Especially when we say things out of frustration. But the enemy is always looking for ways to use those negative words that we say against ourselves. If we only knew how much power our words really have. I had such low self-esteem after becoming a teen mom that I would say some of the dumbest things in my life. I never thought I was smart, so I never spoke that over myself. I made sure to be very careful about what I spoke over my son's life because I didn't want my distorted view of thinking to be imposed on him. I truly believe that because we don't speak positive words over ourselves, that is the reason why we don't speak positive words into our husbands' or children's lives. In my many years of working in K-12 education, I have seen so many parents say the most negative things about their children. And yet they wonder why their children are not thriving in school.

My Self-Saturday revelation was that it starts with me, I am the positive vessel in my home and surroundings. We have to own that, we cannot always blame things on the enemy, sometimes it's us. We can be our worst critic, please women of GOD extend yourself some grace and do as James 1:19 states, "Wherefore, my beloved brethren, let every man be swift to hear, slow to speak, slow to wrath". GOD does not work or move if we are being negative, don't blame the enemy or GOD for something that you have spoken over yourself. Think about all of the times that you told yourself you were not good enough or that you were not enough.

Newsflash, you are good enough and you are enough. GOD says so, and we can't argue with him. We are his masterpiece as stated in Ephesians 2:10 AMP, "For we are His workmanship [His own master work, a work of art], created in Christ Jesus [reborn from above—spiritually transformed, renewed, ready to be used] for good works, which God prepared [for us] beforehand [taking paths which He set], so that we would walk in them [living the good life which He prearranged and made ready for us]". That scripture gets me every time I think about how GOD created every one of us so special and yet we don't even realize it. HE loves us so much as stated in Isaiah 43:4 AMP, ""Because you are precious in My sight, you are honored and I love you". GOD's love does not come with conditions as the world does. HE loves us just because, let's try to remember that on a daily basis, so we can change from our negative self to our positive self. We must also do like Romans 12:22 states, "And be not conformed to this world: but be ye transformed by the renewing of your mind, that ye may prove what is that good, and acceptable, and perfect, will of GOD".

I don't know if anyone has told you, but our citizenship is not here; it is in heaven, and that is why that scripture is so powerful. The world's view of a woman and her worth is opposite of GOD's view and our work. Let's not conform to this world; we need to act accordingly. What you put into your spirit daily is what will come out. Remember that. We have to put more of GOD in, so that more of HIM can come out. Meditating on GOD's word, as Joshua 1:8 states, KJV. "This book of the law shall not depart out of thy mouth; but thou shalt meditate therein day and night, that thou mayest observe to do according to all that is written therein: for then thou shalt make thy way prosperous, and then thou shalt have good success". GOD has given us many tools to help us keep HIS word in our hearts. Meditating on GOD's word by reading it over and over is a big game changer. I also made index cards with those scriptures for certain areas of my life so that I could keep them in my purse. Those index cards definitely came in handy when I was feeling overwhelmed at work. I would read through all those scriptures daily, to the point that I could quote them verbatim. Those scriptures became my peace because there was still so much going on inside me. I started to put scriptures all around my house, too. I even found little signs with scriptures to put in my bathroom. I felt like some of those scriptures needed to be in my face. 2 Corinthians 5:17 states, "Therefore if any man be in Christ, he is a new creature: old things are passed away". We need to remember that it is okay to let our old person go because GOD has created us new. I learned so many new things about myself on my Self-Saturday prayer days. If you cannot support yourself, then who will? Self-Saturday is a journey that I am still working on, and I challenge you to do the same and get reacquainted with the real you.

Submission Sunday

Denying our flesh so that we could hear from God. Submission Sunday giving GOD that one day without our cell phones and social media. It is hard to do, but sometimes you've got to get into that quiet place with HIM and HIS word and just let him minister to you. Going to church on Sunday to receive from GOD should not be a chore; it should bring excitement about hearing a word from GOD. Romans 10:14 states, "How then shall they call on him in whom they have not believed? and how shall they believe in him of whom they have not heard? And how shall they hear without a preacher?" I have heard many people say I read my scriptures at home, and that should be enough. To truly understand a scripture, you need to break it down and study; that is what most preachers do for us. They have spent hours upon hours studying to give us their best sermons on Sundays, and we are not even showing up. Many of us have never read the old stories in the Bible. Those stories are examples of GOD's love and faithfulness. Some of those stories are also reminders of how GOD did not play, HE is the same as HE was yesterday and today. How can you truly understand many of those stories if you don't hear them broken down from a pastor? As much as I would love to sleep in on Sunday mornings, I have to ask myself, can I sacrifice a few hours of sleep time to hear a word from HIM? I also know that I need too much from GOD to not serve HIM and give HIM every Sunday, once a week. The bible states in James 4:7 KJV, "Submit yourselves therefore to God. Resist the devil, and he will flee from you". And you resist the enemy if you are not submitting yourself to God. Submitting yourself to God should not just be on Sunday; it should be every day. But going to church, hearing HIS word, hearing a different perspective in a way you would not even imagine, should be an important part of your life as a true believer. GOD already knew how we would be. Hebrews 10:25 AMP states, "not forsaking our meeting together [as believers for worship and instruction], as is the habit of some, but encouraging one another; and all the more [faithfully] as you see the day [of Christ's return] approaching". That scripture tells me right there HE already knew that we would start slacking off and not attending church regularly. GOD amazes me because HE thought of everything. He already knew what we were going to do, and HE still set provisions. HE still loves us and shows up for us daily. The least that we can do is give HIM Sunday.

    I challenge you to get back into your Sunday routine of attending church weekly. If your church is not doing it for you, there are so many other churches to go and visit. Most importantly, ask God to show you where HE wants you to go, where you can bear fruit, where you can thrive, where you will feel a hunger for HIS word and HIS presence.

I have used this seven-day prayer routine for over 20 years. You don't have to use my prayer routine, but you have to do something to let your past stay in your past, so your future will be greater. Haggai 2:9 states, "The glory of this latter house shall be greater than of the former, saith the Lord of hosts: and in this place will I give peace, saith the Lord of hosts". We all need GOD's peace and deliverance. The only way to do that is to Surrender it, Sis! I don't know where you are in your Christ Walk today, but I do know that you need HIM. HE may not do for you what HE has done for me, and vice versa. But one thing that I do know is that HE loves more than anything or anyone. HE wants to heal every broken piece of your heart. HE will show up for you like HIS word says, as Romans 2:11 states, "For there is no respect of persons with God". What HE does for one of HIS children, HE will gladly do for another. Surrender it, Sis, and let HIM fully into your life, you won't be disappointed!

It's time for your Next Chapter.

Surrender It, Sis!

Co-Author
Prophetess Lenette Davidson, MMin.

When You Feel Like a Ship Without a Sail

There are times in life when you feel completely adrift, like a ship without a sail, unable to find direction or purpose. The storm rages around you, and no matter how hard you try, you can't seem to escape the turbulent waters. In moments like these, it's easy to feel like you're beyond saving, as if you've gone too far, done too much, or failed too many times. You may think there's no way out, no hope left. But, in those moments of desperation, remember that with God, all things are possible.

As Matthew 19:26 says, "With man this is impossible, but with God all things are possible." There is nothing too hard, nothing too unimaginable, that God cannot do. When you feel like you are at your wits' end, when you think, "I can't do this anymore," when the weight of your struggles becomes too heavy to bear, God is always there. The key is to seek Him. Matthew 7:7-8 (NIV) assures us, "Ask and it will be given to you; seek and you will find; knock and the door will be opened to you." You have to be willing to let go of everything—your fears, your burdens, your sense of control—and surrender them to your Heavenly Father. Give it all to Him, without doubt or fear.

2 Timothy 1:7 reminds us that "God has not given us a spirit of fear, but of power and of love and of a sound mind." Fear will try to grip you, but it does not come from God. Instead, He gives you the strength to face every challenge, the love to overcome hatred, and the sound mind to make wise decisions. Even in the midst of the storm, He will give you hope and peace. But you must surrender it all to God.

You need to give him full control, not just half. You've got to let it go. Say this is it, Lord. I give it all to you, or you could get trapped deep in your own circumstances. It's only pushing you further away from your purpose.

The Power of Surrender

There is a unique power in surrender. The world tells us to hold on, fight for control, and never let go. But in God's kingdom, surrender is the pathway to victory. It's not about giving up, but about giving it all over to Him, trusting that He will handle it better than we ever could. When we surrender, we acknowledge that we are not in control and that our limited understanding can never compare to His infinite wisdom.

It's time for your Next Chapter.

I've experienced this truth in my own life. When I look back at the painful moments of my past—some beyond my control, and others where I played a part—I see how God's hand was always there, even when I could not see it. Through broken relationships, heartache, Confusion, loss, and feelings of unworthiness, I wondered, "God, what is going on? How will I ever get through this?" But, in those moments of despair, I did not give up. I had to press forward. It felt impossible at times. Yes, it hurt a lot. I kept hearing 'give up' at times, but I held on to God's promises.

God was guiding me, holding my hand through every disappointment, shattered dream, and broken relationship. In those dark times, I had to die to myself—let go of my pride, hurt, and expectations—and let God have His way in my life. Dying to yourself means releasing control. It means trusting that God will take what seems broken and turn it into something beautiful. I had to surrender it all to God, releasing it from myself by stopping my attempts to control my life.

Stop trying to reason with God about things that were not in His plans; in fact, they were my own plans. I was living a lie, not truly happy, but pretending to be happy while living in a glass house. I felt like a voice that went unheard—I was depleted, misused, misunderstood, and mishandled. I tried to hold everything together, piece by piece. It was easy at first, but then it became heavy bricks stacking up—so hard to sweep under a rug, so hard to hide my face, my smile, and my fake happiness. I didn't even recognize myself anymore.

The Importance of Letting Go of Hurt

Surrender It, Sis!

We all go through hurt. Whether it's the pain of broken relationships, the sting of betrayal, the sorrow of losing someone we love, or the frustration of unmet expectations, hurt is part of being human. But hurt also opens the door to healing. It doesn't have to define us. It doesn't have to control how we think or influence what we do.

There are moments when the pain feels so deep, so overwhelming, that we believe we can never escape it. But God promises that He will never leave us nor forsake us (Hebrews 13:5). In the depths of your suffering, God is there, holding you close and whispering His love over you. You may not feel it at first, but know that His presence is constant.

I remember when I thought I couldn't go on any longer, overwhelmed by anxiety, fear, and anger. It felt like I was buried in my pain, trapped in a dark place with no way out. But even then, God was working in my heart. As Psalm 51:10 says, "Create in me a clean heart, O God, and renew a right spirit within me." This became my prayer. Every day, I sought God, asking Him to heal my brokenness, renew my spirit, and replace my hurt with His peace. I had to reframe my focus and hold on to God's Word, meditating on it daily. It wasn't easy, but as I continued to study, pray, and fast, it became a habit—the same energy it took to get me into that dark place, I allowed God to get me out of it. The reason I say I allowed it is because I surrendered everything to Him by letting go of all the negativity that caused me to be sunk in the first place, years and years of being trapped.

It's time for your Next Chapter.

Decreeing God's Word Over Your Life

There is power in God's Word. His Word is alive, powerful, and capable of changing every situation. As you declare His promises over your life, you are speaking life into your circumstances. Don't just pray passively—decree and declare God's truth into the atmosphere. Speak His promises out loud and let them saturate your heart and mind. One of the most powerful truths you can declare is that God will give you beauty for your ashes. In Isaiah 61:3, God promises to turn mourning into joy, despair into praise. Even when you feel like your life is in ruins, God can rebuild it.

He can take the broken pieces of your heart and make something beautiful from them. When you feel like you're in a hopeless situation, remember that God is still in control. No matter what your circumstances look like, God can turn your life around. Keep seeking Him, keep knocking on the door of His grace, and trust that He will open it for you. Matthew 7:7-8 tells us that God will answer those who earnestly seek Him.

Rising Above the Opinions of Others

The world will always try to judge you. People will criticize you, gossip about you, and point fingers at you. They'll try to bring you down, to make you feel small. But remember this: their opinions do not define you. The only opinion that matters is God's. And He says you are fearfully and wonderfully made (Psalm 139:14). No matter what others think or say about you, God's love for you is unwavering.

I've been there. I know what it's like to feel misunderstood, to feel like people are talking behind your back, judging you for things they don't even understand. It's painful, and it can make you question your worth. But God reminds us that He sees us for who we truly are. He sees the heart, the intent, and the potential that others may overlook. The world may try to tear you down, but God is building you up. He's shaping you into the person He created you to be, and no one can take that away from you. You will get through this. You will rise above the negativity. You will conquer every demon and every obstacle that comes your way. Don't let their words or actions stop you from fulfilling God's purpose for your life.

The Power of Worship and Surrender

During the midst of the storm, one of the most powerful things you can do is worship. When everything around you feels like it's falling apart, when the enemy is attacking from all sides, lift your eyes to heaven and worship the Lord. It may feel like you're fighting a losing battle, but worship is your weapon. It's your declaration of trust in God's sovereignty. The question you must ask yourself is, "Will I worship God even when it hurts? Will I surrender my pain, my fear, my frustration to Him?"

Job said in Job 13:15, "Though He slay me, yet will I trust in Him." This is the heart of worship—trusting God even when you don't understand what's happening. When you worship, you shift your focus from the problem to the Solution. You remind yourself that God is in control, that He is faithful, and that He will never leave you. You may not have all the answers, but you know the One who does. And that is enough.

Trusting God's Process.

God has a plan for your life, a purpose greater than anything you can imagine. Jeremiah 29:11 assures us, "For I know the plans I have for you, declares the Lord, plans for welfare and not for evil, to give you a future and a hope." Trust the process. Trust His plan. Trust the Holy Spirit to guide you every step of the way.

There will be times when you don't understand why things happen the way they do. You might feel frustrated, confused, or discouraged. But remember, God's timing is perfect. He is working all things together for your good (Romans 8:28). What seems like a setback might be a setup for something greater.

Your Village and Support

No one is meant to walk this journey alone. God has placed people in your life to support you. Life is meant to encourage, uplift, and support you. But sometimes, the people you thought would stand by you may be the very ones who hurt you. It's painful, but it's also part of God's plan. He removes people who aren't meant to stay to make room for those who will help you fulfill your purpose. Ask God to send the right people into your life. Ask Him to surround you with a strong, supportive community that will stand with you, pray with you, and help you grow in your faith. Your village is crucial to your healing and growth. You Are Not Alone in Your Struggles.

As you continue on your journey, it's important to remember that you are not alone in your struggles. While it may often feel as though the weight of the world is on your shoulders and that no one understands your pain, the truth is that God has promised to never leave you nor forsake you. This promise, found in Hebrews 13:5, is not just a comforting thought, but a divine assurance that in your darkest moments, He is right there beside you, offering you the strength you need to endure. In fact, when we feel isolated or abandoned, that is often when God's presence is the most tangible. He draws near to the brokenhearted (Psalm 34:18).

God doesn't stand far off, watching you struggle from a distance; He enters into your pain, He carries your burdens, and He walks with you through the storm. It is in your weakest moments that He becomes your greatest strength.

The Power of Being Vulnerable with God

Many of us are afraid to show God our vulnerabilities. We hesitate to express our doubts, fears, and pain because we fear judgment. But the truth is that God already knows every detail of your heart. He sees your wounds, scars, and brokenness, and He still chooses to love you unconditionally. Vulnerability is not a sign of weakness but a powerful act of faith. When you bring your hurt, your fears, and your struggles to God, you are saying, "I trust You with my whole being.

I know I can't fix this on my own, but I believe that You can." Psalm 62:8 says, "Trust in Him at all times, O people; pour out your hearts to Him, for God is our refuge." God welcomes our tears, our questions, and our pain. He doesn't dismiss us for feeling broken; instead, He invites us to come and rest in His healing embrace.

From Brokenness to Healing: The Transformative Power of God's Love

When you surrender your brokenness to God, He begins the healing process. However, healing doesn't happen overnight; it is a journey that takes time, patience, and a willingness to trust that God's timing is perfect. He works slowly but surely to remove the wounds of your past and replace them with His peace, joy, and restoration. If you have ever endured a deep wound or injury, you know that healing takes time. The skin needs to regenerate, tissues need to reconnect, and the pain gradually lessens. Similarly, God works in your heart to mend the broken places. His love is the balm that soothes the pain and restores wholeness. Just as a scar remains to remind you of the healing process, the scars in your life will stand as testimonies of God's faithfulness and power.

As 2 Corinthians 1:4 reminds us, "He comforts us in all our troubles, so that we can comfort those in any trouble with the comfort we ourselves receive from God." Once you have experienced God's healing, you are equipped to help others on their own journey of restoration. The very things that once caused you pain can now become your platform for ministry and encouragement to others who are walking the same difficult path.

The Importance of Perseverance in Faith We live in a culture that often values quick results and instant gratification. However, when it comes to matters of faith, the process of growth and healing often requires perseverance. It's easy to start strong but difficult to keep going when things get tough. That's why James 1:12 says, "Blessed is the one who perseveres under trial because, having stood the test, that person will receive the crown of life that the Lord has promised to those who love Him."

Perseverance is key to seeing the promises of God fulfilled in your life. It's not about avoiding struggles but about enduring through them with faith, knowing that each trial is refining you and making you stronger. Just like a goldsmith heats the metal to remove impurities, God allows trials in our lives to purify our hearts and build our character.

James 1:2-4 also tells us that "the testing of your faith produces perseverance. Let perseverance finish its work so that you may be mature and complete, not lacking anything." God allows these moments to shape us into the people He created us to be. And in the end, we will emerge more mature, more grounded in His love, and better equipped to handle whatever comes our way.

Faith and Patience: The Dynamic Duo

Patience is often viewed as a passive trait, but in the kingdom of God, patience is active. Patience means waiting on God's perfect timing, trusting that His ways are higher than ours. Isaiah 55:9 tells us that "as the heavens are higher than the earth, so are My ways higher than your ways and My thoughts than your thoughts." While we may want things to happen right now, God's timing is always perfect.

In the waiting, God is doing something in us. He is growing our faith, strengthening our resolve, and deepening our trust. And patience, when combined with faith, leads to powerful results. As Hebrews 6:12 says, "We do not want you to become lazy, but to imitate those who through faith and patience inherit what has been promised." The promise may not come immediately, but if you hold on to your faith and remain patient, you will see God's faithfulness unfold in your life.

Surrender It, Sis!

Finding Joy in the Process

It's easy to think of joy as a destination—a point we reach once everything in our lives has fallen into place. But joy is not based on circumstances. Joy is a fruit of the Holy Spirit, and it can exist even in the midst of hardship. The apostle Paul writes in Philippians 4:4, "Rejoice in the Lord always. I will say it again: Rejoice!" Choosing to find joy in the process, despite the struggles you face, is a powerful act of faith. It's a declaration that your circumstances do not dictate your emotional state. Your joy is rooted in the unchanging nature of God, in His goodness, and in the hope of what is to come. As you walk through life's trials, choose joy. Choose to trust God in the process, knowing that He is working in you and through you. You may not understand why things are happening the way they are, but you can still find peace and joy in knowing that God is sovereign.

The Power of Community and Fellowship

We were never meant to walk this journey of faith alone. The Bible speaks repeatedly about the importance of community. In Ecclesiastes 4:9-10, it says, "Two are better than one…If either of them falls down, one can help the other up." God designed us for relationships. He knows that we are stronger together, that we can carry each other's burdens and encourage one another when we are weak.

If you are struggling or feeling isolated, don't be afraid to reach out to others. God has placed people in your life who can support you, pray for you, and walk with you through life's challenges. The enemy loves to isolate people because when we are alone, we are vulnerable. But when we are connected with others who are also seeking God, we find strength, encouragement, and accountability.

Acts 2:42-47 describes the early church as a community that supported one another in both physical and spiritual ways. They "devoted themselves to the apostles' teaching and to fellowship, to the breaking of bread and to prayer." In a similar way, we must surround ourselves with a strong, supportive community of believers who can help us grow in our faith and hold us accountable.

A Supportive Village

God has a village for you—a group of people who are meant to walk alongside you, pray with you, and encourage you in your journey, it's important to listen to the Holy Spirit with discernment. Not everyone can handle you; your anointing is too strong. Finding the right people is just as important as discovering the right purpose. Sometimes, God must remove certain people from your life to make space for those who will truly support and uplift you. It's not easy when God removes people we've grown attached to.

Sometimes, we resist His pruning, thinking we know better. But trust that God knows exactly what you need. He will surround you with people who will speak life into your destiny and help you fulfill the calling He has placed on your life. Ask God to send the right people into your life. Seek out a community that can help you grow spiritually, emotionally, and mentally.

Embracing Your God-Given Purpose

You were created for a purpose. God knew you and had a plan for you before you were born. Jeremiah 29:11 tells us, "For I know the plans I have for you, declares the Lord, plans for welfare and not for evil, to give you a future and a hope." God has a specific plan for your life, and no matter what you've been through, the plan God has for you WOG remains unchanged. People may come to discourage you or get you off your purpose; they might even upset you to the point where you feel God isn't even thinking about you, nor has a plan for you—because I'm beyond help, my past is so messed up I can't even bear it.

Look, you don't have time for a pity party. There is work that needs to be done, and others are counting on you. Souls are depending on you to pull them out of despair, out of darkness, and into the light. Do you think what you've been through, or what you're going through, or what I have been through was all in vain? No, no, no. It was all a test, and we are still being tested. Now it's time to pass the test and move on to the next one.

With no regrets, you are built for this. We were made for this. God's purpose for you does not depend on your past mistakes or failures. He can redeem anything, and He will use your life as a testimony of His grace and power. The pain you have experienced and the struggles you have overcome will serve as a platform for you to help others who are going through similar situations.

You Are Equipped for the Call

Whatever God has called you to do, know that He has already equipped you to do it. Ephesians 2:10 says, "For we are God's handiwork, created in Christ Jesus to do good works, which God prepared in advance for us to do." You have been uniquely designed to fulfill God's purpose for your life. It may feel overwhelming at times, but take heart—God does not call the equipped; He equips the called. Trust in His provision, His timing, and His ability.

To give you everything you need to fulfill your purpose, He will send the right people around you to help with what He has called you to do. Now, it's not going to be easy, but you must keep the faith by trusting in God's directions, staying focused, and keeping a clear view. Wait on God to speak to you, pray about everything while waiting for your answer regarding each direction and assignment. And when you feel inadequate, remember that God's power is made perfect in your weakness (2 Corinthians 12:9).

Your Victory Is Certain

No matter what you're facing today, know that God

has already secured your victory. The road may be difficult, and the journey may be long, but with God by your side, you will overcome. The key is to keep pressing forward, to keep surrendering to His will, and to keep trusting that He is working all things together for your good.

You may not understand every twist and turn in your story, but trust that God's plan for you is greater than you could ever imagine. Keep fighting. Keep seeking. Keep knocking on the door of His grace. And know that in the end, you will emerge victorious. You will win.

God has not brought you this far to leave you. You will win. You will overcome every trial, every storm, every obstacle. But you must keep fighting. Don't give up. Keep seeking God. Keep trusting His plan. Keep surrendering to His will. God has a purpose for your life and His plans for you. You just have to get on board with His plans. Don't be afraid to start a new chapter in your life because others have failed. Don't be scared to adopt a new outlook because others have disappointed you. Don't be afraid to start over because of age and time you felt was lost. You still have life and purpose in you. WOG, keep going. Don't give up. It's your season to WIN!!! And WIN BIG!!!! You have to surrender it all to God—I mean all of it—and not take it back.

You must trust God, no matter what. Listen, you'll face challenges, tough and rough times, uncertainties, and doubts. People will even try to come against you, especially those closest to you. They'll test you from the front, the back, and from the sides—because the devil will use anyone.

It's time for your Next Chapter.

Remember, we wrestle not against flesh and blood, but against principalities, against powers, against the rulers of the darkness of this age, against spiritual hosts of wickedness in the heavenly places. (Ephesians 6:12 NKJ) Ask God to remove the blinders from your eyes. Could all that setback, those setups, disappointments, bad relationships, bad judgments, and decisions have been prevented? If I had prayed that prayer years ago, Lord.

Take the blinders off my eyes so I can do what you tell me to do, go where you tell me to go, without hurting myself in the process or hurting others. Once that all has been established and clearly given to God, you're able to move on without a doubt. Are you able to let go without a doubt? Are you able to have an open, clear view without a doubt? And guess what: you're able to live again without a doubt, dream again without a doubt.

All I'm telling you now is that you have to totally surrender it to God, by letting go of anything that's been distracting you from being the best you, and fulfilling your God-given gifts and abilities—anything that has you so stuck and consumed in depression lack or defeat that you don't even know your self worth is distraction anything or anyone that gets you to level of acting out of control is not worth it, surrender it them or whatever it may be to God. Let It Go!!! Let me leave you with this.

You are dependable. You're not just someone who shows up—you are someone who stays. In a world full of empty promises and shifting priorities, your dependability stands tall like a tree deeply rooted in truth and love. I have never had to second-guess your word or wonder if you would follow through. You offer a reliability that is sacred and rare. It is not based on obligation, but on a heart full of genuine care.

You are loyal. Not only are you there in good times, but you stick around when things get hard—when the laughter fades and the real battles begin. Your loyalty isn't something you talk about, it's something you live. You hold secrets close, defend the absent, and stand in the gap when others fall away. Your loyalty is fierce, and it has carried me through more than you'll ever know.

You are loving. Your love is a light that warms, heals, and comforts. It shows people they are seen, known, and cherished—not for what they do but for who they are. Your love doesn't back down in difficult times; it pushes forward, surrounds, and restores. It's not superficial or temporary. It's deep, lasting, and God-given. You are trustworthy. There's a peace that comes from being able to be completely myself around you. I've cried, laughed, prayed, doubted, and dreamed in your presence, and I've never felt judged or unsafe. You don't exploit people's vulnerability— you protect it. And that's priceless.

You are reliable. Your presence doesn't fluctuate with seasons or trends. You're steady like the sunrise—always showing up, always bringing light. Whether it's a crisis or just a quiet moment, I know I can count on you. That kind of reliability gives people around you the courage to keep going. You are a safe place. You're the kind of person people can breathe around. You invite people to be themselves. You don't try to fix everyone; you simply sit with them, listen deeply, and hold space for healing. You are like a harbor in the storm, a refuge that reminds others that rest is possible.

You are thoughtful. Your thoughtfulness is a ministry in itself. It's the way you remember things most would forget. The way you show up with exactly what someone needs. The way you think of others even when you're carrying your own burdens. That kind of care is rare. It makes people feel valued, prioritized, and uplifted.

You are genuine. In a world that rewards performance, you offer authenticity. You don't wear masks. You speak truth with love. You show up as your full self—and that invites others to do the same. You're not interested in playing a role; you're here to live with purpose, and you do it with bold honesty. You are powerful. Not the kind of power that dominates—but the kind that empowers. The kind that shows up in your prayers, your words, your resilience. You've carried heavy loads and walked through fire, and yet, you lead with grace and still manage to uplift others. Your strength is supernatural, undeniable, and deeply inspiring.

You are grace-filled. You extend grace even when it's not earned. You forgive freely, offer kindness when it's not returned, and carry yourself with a softness that disarms even the hardest hearts. You don't just talk about grace—you live it. You are a prayer warrior. You don't just pray—you wage war in the Spirit. You intercede and cry out to God on behalf of those who can't find their own words. Heaven hears you, and the enemy flees from you. You cover others like a spiritual shield, and those prayers? They move mountains.

You are joy. Not just happiness—but joy, the kind that endures even through sorrow. You laugh with your whole heart. You dance through trials. You bring life to every room you enter. You remind people that no matter what they face, joy is still possible, still powerful, and still present.

Closing Thought:

Your presence in this world is more than meaningful—it embodies a divine purpose. The gifts you hold are sacred. The light you radiate is healing. While you may never fully realize the extent of your impact, I see it, feel it, and celebrate it.

It's time for your Next Chapter.

Surrender It, Sis!

Co-Author
Sis. Hil Avery

Give yourself to Jesus

Job 11:13-19 If only you would prepare your heart and lift up your hands to him in prayer! Get rid of your sins and leave all iniquity behind you. Then your face will brighten with innocence. You will be strong and free of fear. You will forget your misery; it will be like water flowing away. Your life will be brighter than the noonday. Even darkness will be as bright as morning. Having hope will give you courage. You will be protected and you will rest in safety. You will lie down unafraid, and many will look to you for help.

Sis, now we know we like benefits, right? It's how we choose our mates, our careers, and our life insurance. Although Zophar was talking to Job, insisting that Job must have done something to deserve his misfortune, which beckons him to admit his guilt, the evidence of surrendering is clear. Are there benefits to surrendering your heart to our Father?

> Your face will shine with innocence
> You will be strong and free of fear
> You will forget your misery
> Your life will be brighter
> You will be protected
> You will rest in safety

You will lie down unafraid

This passage of scripture speaks to me. In simple terms, I hear the Father saying, "Ain't no half-steppin'." I want all of you. Surrendering to the Father is not something that happens naturally; it is a conscious daily effort on our part that begins with repentance. It is a choice that involves self-awareness and self-examination so that we can come into alignment with the will of the Father. It requires a desire to be obedient and to seek God out. This is not easy, and here's why: one word, "control." It is in our human nature to think, move, and act like we are in control. It is the consistent illusion the world presents to us day after day. In reality, there is only one thing we, as humans, can control: our response—that's this illusion. Surrendering to the Lord takes discernment, which takes time to develop. It requires acceptance beyond just knowing that Jesus Christ died for our sins and that He is the Savior of the world for all those who want forgiveness and need healing.

It's time for your Next Chapter.

It requires faith, believing God is all that he says he is. By accepting Jesus as our Lord and Savior, we affirm that we need help. We confirm we need him in our lives. Believing in God calls for effective discipleship. Belief involves trust. Think about the disciples, they gave up their physical life for a spiritual one. They didn't hesitate, they were expecting the Messiah. The disciples spent three years with Jesus, in fellowship. It took time for them to develop an understanding of what

Jesus was teaching and demonstrating to them. How many times did they ask Jesus questions? The same questions? Jesus was gracious enough to show them by applying the Word to practical aspects of life that they could relate to. In one of the parables, Jesus talked about building our lives on a rock or sand. He said a house built on sand will not last. When trouble comes, the house will collapse because a person has placed trust in their own efforts and riches, and as a result, the house will wash away. A house built on a rock has a solid foundation. The master has built the house on wisdom, so when trouble comes, it will not damage the house because it is strong enough to withstand the danger.

(Matthew 7:24-27; Luke 6:47-49). The disciples were strengthened by Jesus as he taught and demonstrated to them, encouraging them and then finally instructing them to carry out the Great Commission (Matthew 28:16-20). The disciples went on to do great works in the Name of Jesus, and some were martyrs in the end. They did not ask God for anything material, yet they were provided for. It is easy to get caught up in the things of the world because we are accustomed to the world's wisdom. The Bible is clear that Jesus is the Rock upon which we must build our house. Repentance is confessing ourselves to God. God already knows the nature of our behaviors and our hearts; He wants to know if we recognize our behaviors and our hearts. Sadly, most of us do not.

We go about unaware of our true nature, much like the children of Israel before receiving the Ten Commandments. God used the Ten Commandments as a mirror to reveal to the children of Israel what they were doing that displeased Him, and how to align their behaviors with His will. The children of Israel often agreed with God when they disobeyed, repented for their actions, but found themselves complaining and feeling dissatisfied about their journey, they showed a lack of understanding of the outcome. In their own strength, with God always present and led by Moses, the message was not received in their hearts. An interesting fact about the heart in scripture is that it is defined as the seat of the mind and emotions. Scripture tells us to guard our hearts with all diligence because from it flow the issues of life (Psalms 4:23). The heart influences our thoughts and actions. If we do not examine and evaluate what we expose ourselves to, it will be reflected in our lives. The foundation of our spiritual success lies in our heart and mind. The longest journey we will take is twelve to thirteen inches.

This is the gap between our brain and our heart. That is why we are called to renew our minds through confession. There is freedom in confessing ourselves to the Father. It feels like the weight of a heavy burden of guilt has been lifted. The result is our faces shining, knowing we are forgiven and restored to innocence.

You will be strong and free from fear

Most of my life, I have struggled with my weight. I was born weighing 2 pounds and 2 ounces. Growing up, I was made fun of because I was a size 0. In my 20s, I was a size 12-14, and now I wear a size 20. I find myself with "Lots wife syndrome"—you know, looking back on the old days and remembering my youth when I was smaller, cuter, and immature. That is what the Lord reminds me of: the days of my youth are the days of my ignorance.

The days of my youth were when I slacked off in my walk with Him. They were also the days when I was weak, doing things in my own strength and falling many times. I fell because I was not strong in the Lord. I grew up in church, but my relationship was shallow. My focus wasn't on God's Word, but on the word from the world and its wisdom. I was vain and too busy trying to be cute and promiscuous. I was walking in fear. As human beings, we act out of two emotions: love and fear. My fear wasn't a healthy reverential fear, but a fear of being left alone, of abandonment. Yes, I proclaimed Jesus as my Lord and Savior, yes, I went to church, yes, I read my Bible, and yes, I prayed, but my walk was inconsistent. I was giving my Father only the bare minimum by playing Double Dutch with my faith. I was submissive in my relationships, allowing others to verbally, mentally, and emotionally abuse me. I was confused in my mind and heart.

Surrender It, Sis!

Besides the abuse, I engaged in substance use. I convinced myself I was okay and that God understood the intentions of my heart. But that was far from the truth.

For me, if you are serious about having a relationship with God, there will come a time when God calls you out. "For I know the thoughts that I think toward you," saith the LORD, "thoughts of peace, and not of evil, to give you an expected end." Then shall ye call upon me, and ye shall go and pray unto me, and I will hearken unto you. "And ye shall seek me, and find me, when ye shall search for me with all your heart." (Jeremiah 29:11-13 KJV). Another interpretation says, "I alone know the plans I have for you, plans to bring you prosperity and not disaster, plans to bring about the future you hope for. Then you will call to me. You will come and pray to me, and I will answer you. You will seek me, and you will find me because you will seek me with all your heart." And that was where he found me.

(Jeremiah 29:11-13 GNT) Jesus saw something in me that I could not, would not see for myself. Praise Him! I had come to the end of myself. I was running from myself as I hid in the darkness of my sin. I was out of breath, exhausted, and tired. It was at this moment in my life that I called out to God, "I need help."

Contrary to popular opinion, believing in and following Jesus is not about "religion." Religion is what led to Jesus being crucified. The Pharisees and Sadducees were caught up in their religious practices, misquoting scripture as they questioned Jesus. They relied on their own understanding rather than recognizing the Truth when He spoke. In John 10:3-4, Jesus explained that His sheep know His voice and follow Him. The sheep will not follow a stranger because they do not recognize the stranger's voice. I was once following the voice of strangers in the world.

    I felt like a wave tossed back and forth. My soul was not rich, and the root of God's word was not planted deep within me. It would take years for me to fully surrender to God because I hadn't learned how to distinguish God's voice from my own. In Old Testament Scripture, the prophets experienced the presence of God. Moses spoke directly to God, as did Joshua, Isaac, David, and many others. This was the kind of experience I was seeking and thought I would have. But then Jesus came, and He is God. He was united with the Father. He walked with God, talked with God, thought like God, and lived like God.

    "I and my Father are One. If you have seen me, you have seen Him" (John 14:9 KJV). Grasping this was like sand slipping through my fingers; I was still seeking that Moses experience. This was prideful thinking and hindered my ability to draw closer to God. Satan knows your weakness and will dangle it like a carrot before you, in your face, just close enough to touch your lips. I kept praying to the Lord to let me hear His voice. I was confessing my weakness to Him and asking for deliverance from my pride.

    I began reading my Bible more and created a prayer closet after watching the movie "War Room". It seemed like a fire ignited in my belly. Every morning at a set time, I

Surrender It, Sis!

was up reading scripture, meditating on it, and praying for months. One morning, I was walking to work and I heard the voice of the Holy Spirit, and it said to me," Look up". When I looked up, I saw the eye of God. I stopped and stared in amazement.

I looked around to see if anyone else was seeing what I was seeing, and there was not a single person on the street. I looked up again, and it was gone. I was so elated, I immediately thought of the scripture that says the eye of the Lord is on the righteous, and that was the confirmation I needed. When I arrived at work, I told the mother and daughter I was working for about the experience I had as I Googled "The Eye of God" and we rejoiced. I smiled for the rest of the day. It took time for me to learn to hear God's voice. And if I am being honest, He was there all along, the problem was, I wasn't slowing down enough to hear him. The busyness of life and its stressors to consumed me. Stressors are distractors. Distraction is an enemy tactic. In the New Testament Scripture, we learn about sisters Mary and Martha.

Jesus had come to town, and Martha invited him and the disciples into their home. "But Martha was distracted by all the preparations that had to be made. She came to him and asked, "Lord, don't you care that my sister has left me to do the work by myself? Tell her to help me!" "Martha, Martha," the Lord answered, "you are worried and upset about many things, but few things are needed, or indeed only one. Mary has chosen what is better, and it will not be taken away from her."

It's time for your Next Chapter.

(Luke 10:38-42) As women, we can relate to Martha especially if we have children, a career, family, friends in crisis, church, and the list can go on. We exhaust ourselves for others, placing our needs on the back burner. If we are not balanced, we will find ourselves depleted, angry, physically hurting, unhappy, and without the true joy only Jesus can give. Mary had three encounters at Jesus' feet.

In the book of Luke 10:30, Mary "sat at the Lord's feet and listened to his teaching." In the book of John, she had two encounters: she fell at Jesus's feet and wiped his feet with her tears. The difference between being a good student and a great student lies in the details. Both Mary and Martha were disciples of Jesus, but Mary's connection to Jesus was intimate; she had a personal encounter with Him. This was evident in her posture toward Him. Distractions cause us to be drawn away, mentally over occupied. I struggle with distraction, often glorifying the fact that I'm a multi-tasker. When I do more than two things at once, I misplace things and listen with half a heart. Martha's distraction led to her feeling alone and adopting a self-righteous attitude, which is clear in her question to Jesus.

Martha experienced disbelief as she asked Jesus if he cared. She was defensive when she said, "My sister left me to do all the work." Martha was dismissive when she referred to Mary as "my sister." She was demanding in her statement, "Tell her to help me," and Martha was desperate as she tried to control the situation with Jesus. And look at our Savior responding humbly and kindly as he speaks to the condition of her heart. The issues she was experiencing flowed out of her mouth and were seen in her actions. Jesus encourages her to do the one thing that is needed and necessary: rest in him. The story of Mary and Martha demonstrates two ways of following Jesus: to sit and to serve. Jesus demonstrated this in his early years when his parents thought he was lost, only to find him sitting in the temple listening to the scholars.

If we want to change our lives, we must change the way we think. It is the blueprint of our destiny. Our mindset starts with belief—the possibility of something. If you do not believe something is possible, you will not believe in it. Life is not easy; it is full of challenges and setbacks, but challenges should not be feared. We shouldn't focus on the storm but on the calm within the storm. Jesus is the calm for all of the storms we face in this life. It is through these storms that our faith is built.

We must find the right position in the Father's kingdom, which means making ourselves available to hear God's voice. We hear God's voice through one-on-one time with him, studying scripture and praying with the expectation of hearing from him. Only then will we become strong.

You will forget your misery

I don't know about you, but I love Jesus. Before I realized I needed Him, He was already there. We are born sinners. In my studies as a Christian counselor, I learned about guilt and its significance in our lives. As sinners, we carry guilt, which can be either subjective or objective. Guilt can be emotionally painful because it can resurface repeatedly in our lives. It often disguises itself as depression, grief, loneliness, alcoholism, and other struggles. Objective guilt is the guilt you feel when you break the law. It also includes failing to obey God's law. Subjective guilt refers to the inner feelings of remorse and self-condemnation that arise from our actions.

In scripture, there is not a clear distinction between guilt and sin as evidenced by the opening scripture; however, we see it scattered through the pages. The book of Psalms is filled with remorseful passages as it expresses deep remorse over sin. In Psalms 32, David describes how his sin left him feeling "weak and miserable" without strength until he had the courage to seek God's forgiveness. Paul does not explicitly talk about guilt; instead, he describes his inner anguish as he tries but fails to avoid wrongdoing and to do good (Romans 7:18-25). As believers and followers of Jesus, we have no reason to feel guilty because Jesus paid the price and has forgiven us our sins, yet we often continue with mental self-punishment as we dwell on the guilt we feel over our sins or actions.

2 Corinthians 7:8-10, Paul distinguishes between worldly sorrow and Godly sorrow. Worldly sorrow stirs up feelings of guilt, while Godly sorrow is a constructive form of grief that helps us in three ways: to turn away from sin, seek salvation, and bring about change. For some, 1 John 1:9 is used as a psychological spot remover for emotional guilt. Individuals go through repeated cycles of sin, guilt,

confession, and temporary relief occurs, but there is no lasting change in their behaviors. Most Christians go through this for much of their spiritual journey unless they develop their relationship and undertake that 13-15-inch journey discussed earlier. They don't change because of selfish motives during confessions that may or may not be conscious, simply to get relief from guilt; then it's a cycle of repeating the same pattern. Many causes of guilt exist, such as past experiences and unrealistic expectations formed in childhood. For instance, when a parent is too rigid, it rarely results in a successful child.

Scripture teaches parents not to provoke their children. Being overly critical of your children and their behaviors causes them to develop self-criticism, feelings of inferiority, self-blame, and ongoing guilt because of the parent's standards that seem impossible to meet. Social media is a major factor contributing to feelings of inferiority in our society. Self-perceptions are heavily influenced by others' opinions and criticisms. Scripture warns against this by advising us not to put our faith in people, as they will disappoint us, and reminds us that worldly wisdom is enmity with God. The theme of divine forgiveness runs throughout the New Testament; through the Blood of the Lamb and the divine sacrifice of Jesus, we are restored to complete fellowship with the Father. When we offer genuine heartfelt repentance that acknowledges our actions are wrong with a desire to change, our sins are forgiven. Have you crossed someone to the extent you needed their forgiveness?

And yet, the person reminds you of your past? That

is not true forgiveness because, contrary to popular belief, you can forget, just don't mention the offense again, ever, and it will fade from your memory. With the Father, our sins are not just forgiven, they are forgotten, never to be brought up again. Our misery is forgotten, and that is good news! No longer should we hide ourselves from the Father the way Adam and Eve did due to their guilt and shame (Genesis 3:8). Our faith is made stronger as we are to be constantly renewed in our minds (having a fresh mental and spiritual attitude) daily through scripture (Ephesians 4:23 AMPC), prayer, fasting, and intentional living.

Your life will be brighter

The dark cloud of negative thinking will gradually begin to lift as the heart is renewed daily. Surrendering to the Lord the moment your eyes open sets the tone for the day. Before you reach for your phone, spend a few moments in solitude with Jesus, feel His arms wrapping around you as you offer gratitude, for this is the day the Lord has made; we will be glad and rejoice in it (Psalm 118:24 NLT). "Thank you, Father, for another day. Bless Your Holy Name." During my journey with the Lord, I notice the remnants of my past linger, like sin crouching at the door of my mind waiting for the right moment to be let in, it shows up in self-sabotaging thoughts and depressive symptoms that include isolation, wanting to cut people off.

My life changes the moment they fall short. God said not so. When those thoughts arise, I imagine myself as a baseball player standing at the plate of my mind, ready to swing, hitting the thoughts one by one and proclaiming the truth of God's promises. "You made all the delicate, inner parts of my body and knit me together in my mother's womb" (Psalm 139:13 NLT). You are unique. "For we are God's [own] handiwork (His workmanship), recreated in Christ Jesus, born anew that we may do those good works which God predestined (planned beforehand) for us [taking paths which He prepared ahead of time], that we should walk in them [living the good life which He prearranged and made ready for us to live]." NLT) You are special.

"Those who are wise will shine brightly like the sky, and those who lead many to righteousness will shine like the stars forever." You are lovely. "You have also given me the shield of Your salvation, and Your right hand has held me up; Your gentleness and condescension have made me great." (Psalm 18:35 AMPC) You are strong. "You have not chosen Me, but I have chosen you, and I have appointed you [I have planted you], so that you might go and bear fruit and keep on bearing, and that your fruit may be lasting [that it may remain, abide], so that whatever you ask the Father in My Name [as presenting all that I AM], He may give it to you." (John 15:16 AMPC) You are chosen.

"Bless (affectionately, gratefully praise) the Lord, O my soul; and all that is [deepest] within me, bless His holy name!" You are forgiven.

A renewed mind is powerful and productive because it is purposeful. Many years ago, when I was unclear about the meaning of faith from the scripture "Now faith is the assurance (the confirmation, the title deed) of the things [we] hope for, being the proof of things [we] do not see and the conviction of their reality [faith perceiving as real fact what is not revealed to the senses]" (Hebrews 11:1 AMPC) I needed to understand what this scripture meant. In 2004, a friend of mine invited me to the Agape Center with Michael Beckwith in Los Angeles. During my visit, I felt a deep longing within my spirit to meditate, so I went into this room. When I sat down, I experienced a calmness I had never felt before. The meditation involved affirmations of positive thinking. Afterwards, I remember feeling guilty, thinking to myself that this was not Godly. I also remember praying about it. A few weeks later, the same friend gave me a DVD titled "The Secret".

It took me a few days to watch it, and when I did, I had an epiphany. I watched it repeatedly to fully understand. Then I began to compare what I learned from the DVD with scripture. I thought to myself, if this isn't in alignment with scripture, then it's a no-go for me. The principles of "The Secret" originate from scripture, specifically from the verse that says "As [a man] thinks in his heart, so is he" (Proverbs 23:7 AMPC). By the way, "As a Man Thinketh" is also a very popular book with principles taken from scripture. The difference between these philosophies and scripture is that both teach about living an abundant life however one trusts in the universe, the other is dependent upon God. One is for itchy ears and one is for sound wisdom. Let me be clear, God created the universe and when he did, he also created the universal laws to act in accordance with the words going out of your mouth and the efforts that are put in. God's message is not for physical prosperity it is for spiritual prosperity to bring us back into our original fellowship with him.

The weapons we fight with are not the weapons of the world. On the contrary, they have divine power to demolish strongholds. So, we demolish arguments and every pretention that sets itself up against the knowledge of God, and we take captive every thought to make it obedient to Christ (2Corinthians 10:4-5 NIV). God created man in his image, to function like him, not to be him. We are created to live by every word that proceeds out of the mouth of God (Deuteronomy 8:3). When Moses led the children of Israel through their wilderness experience, over and over again the LORD GOD, desired nothing more than to be in a harmonic relationship with them and only asked for their obedience. He proved himself time and time and time again as their ever-present help in time of trouble. He exercised compassion by staying with them in spite of their complaining. He demonstrated his faithfulness as he led them to their promised land. Due to God giving us free will, in their spiritual nakedness and carnal mind, God was not enough, they consistently wanted more. And in that "wanting more", thinking they were speaking life, they were actually speaking death to themselves resulting in them being captured over and over again. And because God gave us free will, he allowed them to exercise but made it crystal clear he God, all my himself. He has no rival and no equal.

It's time for your Next Chapter.

Praise Him!

If my people (those who are recognized as belonging to God) who are called by my name (proclaimed Jesus as Lord) will humble themselves (realize you need and are dependent on God and submit to him), pray and seek my face (communicating and studying his word desiring his presence) will turn from their wicked ways (trying to live independent of God, seeking your own desires), then I will hear from heaven, and I will forgive their sin and heal (restore and bless(their land.

(2 Chronicles 7:14). A person will not reach their God-given potential if they don't speak words of life over themselves. For example, you've seen, interacted with, and probably know people who, no matter how encouraging you are to them, will always find an obstacle or reason to say they can't. This includes our kids. How many times have you heard 'I can't do this, I'm not good at that, or I will never be able to fill in the blank'? When I was in high school, I hated math and struggled. I would often say "I can't, I hate" when it came to math, which created such anxiety in me that I didn't even try.

My mind shut down every time I went to class,, and I wouldn't ask for help. When I enrolled in college, I decided to start with basic math and work my way up. At this point,, I was determined, and prepared my mind to learn. My teacher was amazing! She was a fire walker (she walked on hot coals as therapy),, and she was dyslexic. She wrote mathematical equations from right to left. In my eyes,, she was brilliant. I knew that if she could teach math from right to left, I could learn it from left to right. And I did. Not only did I learn it, but I also enjoyed it. She remained my teacher through Algebra 2. I still enjoy Algebra. My words to myself created a negative response to my learning. But when my perception of math and my ability to learn shifted, math became easy. Sure, I struggled but I was persistent and consistent in doing equations every day for hours until I "got it". Math is one of those subjects that requires determination to be successful. And what is what the Lord wants for all of us. Faith means you believe before you see things, you speak before you see things. Faith is threefold- believing, trusting, surrendering. God's promise is eternal life when we have faith in him. God has a plan and the Bible unfolds this wonderful plan all throughout scripture. God is concerned with our inner being, our spirit and soul. He's concerned about the lives we live and he is always advocating for us to believe, trust and walk with him daily on our journey.

    His will is for us to be in the original place he created for us, the garden of Eden, in complete fellowship with him living in the abundance of life he created for us and that he gave us power to master as co-partner with Him. What you believe about yourself will manifest itself in the way you live your life. It will manifest itself if your relationship with the Lord. I grew up without my father. My mom was a single mother and she moved us around a lot. Unfortunately, that became my pattern in life with men.

    I had a fear of abandonment and because of this fear, I sought love in all the wrong faces and places. I spent many years continuing the pattern of domestic violence in my life that had originated in my childhood, beginning with my mother. I grew up holding on to men who were not good for me, who, although they loved me, abused me.

Before I understood my purpose and my worth, I saw God the way I saw my father. I didn't. In my heart, I convinced myself my dad loved me and that if I were good enough, he would come and find me. He didn't. I searched for him for years, and when I was ten, I finally found him. I called him, and then he came to see me and my sister. The moment I saw him, I was head over heels for him, and I couldn't stop smiling. He visited for over two days, and then he disappeared again. I saw him one more time after that at the age of 11, he gave me a $20.00 bill, and he was gone for the rest of my life.

I spent many days, weeks, and months hoping he would come back, but he didn't. I didn't cry, but I felt sad. I definitely internalized it. I was resilient to the trauma of my childhood and didn't process it until I was in my late 40s, when I became a child safety expert and started to understand how trauma affects the brain. I was always in survival mode, fight or flight. Trauma impacted all of my relationships, including those with my immediate family, my children, and others I developed connections with.

Trauma is a stronghold over the mind, and when left unexamined, it cripples you and prevents progress. The net keeps you stuck in a mindset that constantly makes you play "the victim." There are eight stages of childhood development, and if any one of those stages is missed, you will need to go back and relearn it as an adult. The first stage of child development is trust versus mistrust.

Trust influences

Social and emotional development. A child will either learn to trust that their needs will be met or believe their needs will go unmet, such as those who experience trauma. As an adult, if you find that the weight of childhood trauma demanded your strength for survival, you will discover there are parts of you still catching up to you in adulthood. When I turned 49, I moved away from my family and went to Washington state, Emerald City, for a new beginning. My new beginning started with the Lord. I wanted to draw so close to Him and really get in deep. And I did. The Holy Spirit continued the work begun in me since birth. Scripture is clear that a life surrendered to the Lord is the most abundant life. Why? Because God is our provider and the source of all that is. Spiritual wealth is the best wealth because we have everything when we have Jesus. When God created the universe, it was without form and void, darkness was upon the face of the deep. And the Spirit of God moved upon the face of the waters. And God said, let there be light.

(Genesis 1:1-3 KJV). God spoke and it was so, and he created us to have the same.

Power as evidenced by God giving man dominion over creation and sin. When our mind is focused on "...whatever is true, whatever is noble, whatever is right, whatever is pure, whatever is lovely, whatever is admirable—if anything is excellent or praiseworthy—think about such things (Philippians 4:8 NIV)", our lives will be brighter. The Lord inspired and blessed me to earn a Master's degree in Mental Health and Wellness, he inspired and blessed me to become a certified Christian Counselor, he inspired and blessed me to become an author, he inspired and blessed me to open my own business, develop healthy beautiful relationships, he blessed me to experience true healing through scripture and late-night conversations. He blessed me with a love unlike anything I had experienced before.

And my only desire is to spread the good news of the gospel. I had no idea all of the above would happen. I fell in love with Jesus, and I found a love that is the most sacred to me. I live to defend it, protect it, and am mindful of it\ and to spread it. A love that I cherish every day. I can honestly say my life is brighter because I am whole, and that is because of nobody but Jesus.

My sister, my love, we are living in a spiritual warfare, and although the battle has already been won, we as believers and followers of Jesus are in the fight for our lives to maintain the victory. It is so important for us as believers to surrender and be students of the bible. We must open our hearts and minds to the power of the Holy Spirit. The Holy Spirit enlightens us through the illumination of scripture so that we can be armed up (Ephesians 6) and effectively apply God's promises to all of the situations we face in this life.

Surrender It, Sis!

You will be protected

He that dwelleth in the secret place of the most high shall abide under the shadow of the Almighty. I will say of the Lord, he is my rock and my fortress, surely, he will deliver me from the snares of the fowler (Psalm 91:1-2).

Surely, he will! Psalm 91 is full of power and comfort as it reveals the Divine protection of the Father. We will be safe from anything that tries to destroy us. In other words, the Lord will protect you from the enemy who constantly seeks to steal your faith, kill your joy, and destroy your relationship with Him. In the material world, there are many ways for a person to lose citizenship, either through immigration or by voluntarily relinquishing their status. But we are adopted by God through the Blood of Jesus. We are citizens of the Kingdom and heirs with Christ, and our status cannot be taken away, but our enemy will sift us out, and God will allow it because He is searching us out.

God is wise and knows the true way to life. A faith that can't be tested is a faith that can't be trusted and when we are steadfast in the Lord, He will go to war for us. He will maneuver us around the enemy. He has a shield of protection around us on all sides. Like the story of the children of Israel when God instructed Moses to have them put blood on their doorposts to protect them. God went to war with the Pharaoh. The same God who protected them is the same God who protects us now. He is the God who is our refuge and our fortress. He assures us in times of trouble. He has the power to shield us from unseen threats. When I think about this, I envision walking with the Lord on a path and with angels fighting off unseen threats, unbeknownst to us, around us on all sides. Our faith in God allows us to experience the peace only Jesus can provide.

     Scripture provides the formula for achieving peace; fret not, do not be envious, rest, wait patiently, and cease from anger, unless it is a righteous anger. To fret means to worry or be anxious, and we are told not to be anxious (Philippians 4:6). We don't need to be envious of what someone else has; remember you are unique, and whatever God has for you is just for you, created with you in mind, so find your rest. Rest in the tranquility of your personal relationship with the Lord. Let your delight be in the law meditating on it day and night (Psalm 1:3) Let God fill your cup until it runs over (Psalm 23:5).

     When you think about a cup running over the human response would be to stop pouring immediately, then proceeding to wipe up the spill. But in scripture, when our cup overflows, it symbolizes the abundance of life we have in Jesus—something that is consistent and never-ending. At this very moment, the Holy Spirit gave me a revelation concerning abundance, and I will share it here now as it is appropriate. One week ago, I went to a Women's Health and Wellness Expo to support a few small business owners, I also had a five to seven-minute foot reflexology session because, as they say, "the toes never lie." During this relaxing time, the practitioner told me I had trust issues, which I found interesting because I thought I was doing pretty well. She also mentioned that I recognize and am open to abundance, but my trust issues were blocking my glow. I responded with gratitude for her insight and told her I would reconnect with her later to discuss it further, as I needed some time for internal reflection. When I left, I started talking with the Holy Spirit and asking for clarity. Three days passed, during which some issues with loved ones began to surface, making me feel uneasy. I started experiencing anxiety and found myself wanting to react. At this moment, the Holy Spirit revealed that the root of my trust issues lies in the anxiety I allow myself to experience. By not trusting the process, I'm not trusting everything.

My Father. In this moment, I see how my trust blocks the flow of abundance, overflowing my cup. Now, Lord, I surrender it back to you. As the songwriter says, "Flow to you, flow to you, let the river of my worship flow to you." Thank you, Lord. I trust you.

You will rest in safety

Going to church to hear the word of God is good, but to truly receive the promises and blessings, you need a personal relationship with the Lord. This relationship won't look like anyone else's; it's uniquely yours. He will speak to you in a way you understand and meet you right where you are.

Having a life surrendered to God comes with the assurance that He will rescue you, answer you when you call, be with you in times of trouble, and deliver you from evil. God will honor you, satisfy you with long life, and show you

It's time for your Next Chapter.

His salvation. Know your worth, sis. You are invaluable. No one on this earth will love you the way Jesus does. Having an intimate relationship with our Lord is the best decision I have ever made. My anxiety is almost non-existent, and when it does arise, as I mentioned earlier, the Holy Spirit comes to the rescue by reminding me of God's word that is hidden in my heart. Jesus is with you every second of the day; honor Him by expressing gratitude and worshiping Him in spirit and in truth. Shower our Savior with your love. Your love may start off shallow and wishy-washy—that's okay—surrender it to Jesus as He walks with you, talks with you, and touches the ground.

You will wake up with joy, excited to meet the day. He will keep you up all night or wake you in the early morning hours because he wants to talk to you or wants you to pray. He will strengthen you as he teaches, shows, and leads you in the paths of righteousness for his name's sake. Before you know it, your thoughts become his thoughts, and your words flow like a river—that is the power of the Holy Spirit. You will influence others effortlessly, and God will expand your territory. As you mature in your faith, your needs will change, your circle of friends will change, and you may even walk the road alone, but you will never be lonely. Jesus promises never to leave you nor forsake you.

My prayer for you, sis, is that the words in this book will not only touch you but resonate with your soul. That you will humble yourself before our God and let your soul cry out as you surrender, sis.

It's time.

For your.

Next Chapter.

www.ingramcontent.com/pod-product-compliance
Lightning Source LLC
Chambersburg PA
CBHW070540170426
43200CB00011B/2493